Monumental Legacy

HAMPI

Anila Verghese

OXFORD
UNIVERSITY PRESS

OXFORD
UNIVERSITY PRESS

YMCA Library Building, Jai Singh Road, New Delhi 110001

Oxford University Press is a department of the University of Oxford. It furthers the
University's objective of excellence in research, scholarship, and education
by publishing worldwide in

Oxford   New York
Athens   Auckland   Bangkok   Bogota   Buenos Aires   Cape Town
Chennai   Dar es Salaam   Delhi   Florence   Hong Kong   Istanbul
Karachi   Kolkata Kuala Lumpur   Madrid   Melbourne   Mexico City   Mumbai
Nairobi   Paris   Sao Paolo   Shanghai   Singapore   Taipei   Tokyo   Toronto   Warsaw

with associated companies in

Berlin   Ibadan

Oxford is a registered trade mark of Oxford University Press
in the UK and in certain other countries

Published in India
By Oxford University Press, New Delhi

ISBN   0 19 565433 1

The publishers, series editor, and authors can accept
no responsibility for any loss or inconvenience caused
by any error or misinformation in the Series,
though every care is taken in compiling the books.

Printed in India at Pauls Press, New Delhi 110020
and published by Manzar Khan, Oxford University Press
YMCA Library Building, Jai Singh Road, New Delhi 110001

Series Editor's Preface

There are 690 sites on the World Heritage list, as on December 2000, 'inscribed' as properties by the World Heritage Committee of UNESCO. These sites are 'considered to be of outstanding value to humanity', and the preservation of this shared heritage concerns all of us. India has been an active member-state on the World Heritage Forum since 1977, and is one of the countries on the list, with 22 World Heritage Sites. Of these, 17 are recorded as cultural sites, while the rest are natural sites.

I am delighted that the Oxford University Press is publishing brief books on each of the 17 cultural sites, under its series titled *Monumental Legacy*. So far, the following cultural sites in India have been listed as World Heritage sites:

Ajanta Caves (1983), Ellora Caves (1983), Agra Fort (1983), Taj Mahal (1983), Sun Temple, Konarak (1984), Group of Monuments at Mahabalipuram (1985), Churches and Convents of Goa (1986), Group of Monuments at Khajuraho (1986), Group of Monuments at Hampi (1986), Fatehpur Sikri (1986), Group of Monuments of Pattadakal (1987), Elephanta Caves (1987), Brihadisvara Temple, Thanjavur (1987), Buddhist Monuments at Sanchi (1989),

Humayun's Tomb (1993), Qutb Minar and its Monuments (1993), and the Darjeeling Himalayan Railway (1999).

There is scope, indeed, for recognition of many more Indian sites in future on the World Heritage list. I am sure that as, and when, these are declared as World Heritage Sites, they will be included under the Monumental Legacy Series of the Oxford University Press.

The Oxford University Press, in consultation with me, have invited experts in the field to contribute small books, addressed to general readers, on each of these 17 World Heritage Sites in India. These books obviously differ from cheap tourist books and glossy guide books and, at the same time, also from specialized monographs. Their importance lies in the fact they are written by authorities on the subject, to enable visitors to see the monuments in proper perspective.

My sincere thanks to all the authors of the Series and to the editorial staff at the OUP. Their constant support and enthusiasm are much appreciated.

October 2001   D.D.

Contents

Illustrations

Figures

Photographs
Black and White:

Colour   (between pp. 46–7)

Preface and Acknowledgements

This book on Hampi-Vijayanagara is a labour of love, the fruit of sixteen years of visits to and research on the site. I have carried out extensive and intensive field work at Hampi, which has resulted in three books and several research papers. These, however, are of interest primarily to the specialist. Hence the present work, which is aimed at the general reader and visitors to the site.

*

It is my privilege that the publication of this book coincides with the second centenary of the visit to Hampi (in 1799–1800) of Colonel Colin Mackenzie, the first antiquarian to make a survey of the monuments and prepare a site map, and also with the centenary of the publication of Robert Sewell's pioneering work on Vijayanagara, A *Forgotten Empire*. I should like to dedicate this volume to them and to other scholars whose efforts have brought this formerly little-known site to the notice of both scholars and the public.

I would like to acknowledge the help, support, and encouragement that I have received from a number of persons and institutions.

I am grateful to the past and present Directors of the Karnataka State Directorate of Archaeology and Museums and to their officers and staff at Hampi for the hospitality extended to me since 1983 at the Directorate's site camp. I owe a very special debt of gratitude to the Directors of the Vijayanagara Research Project, Dr John M. Fritz and Dr George Michell, not only for all the assistance that I have received from them over the years, but also for the maps and drawings reproduced in this volume. I thank John Gollings for the colour plates (the black and white photographs are from my personal collection and most of them were taken by me). I should also like to convey my sincere thanks to Dr Anna L. Dallapiccola of the Project. Lively discussions on the site with members of the Project and our mutual sharing of many new insights have enriched my understanding of Hampi-Vijayanagara. I am grateful to the Management of Sophia College for permitting me to carry on with my ongoing research on Vijayanagara. Above all, I thank my publishers, Oxford University Press, and the general editor of the series, Dr Devangana Desai, for giving me this opportunity to share my enthusiasm for Hampi with others.

October 2001   Anila Verghese

ONE

Introduction

Hampi is a village situated on the southern bank of the Tungabhadra river in the Hospet *taluka* of Bellary district, Karnataka. This site served as the capital of the Vijayanagara kingdom from the mid-fourteenth century to 1565 AD. As the seat of a kingdom that extended from the Arabian sea to the Bay of Bengal and from the Deccan plateau to the tip of the peninsula, Vijayanagara was presented by its rulers as a showpiece of imperial magnificence and the greatest of all medieval Hindu capitals that came to be celebrated throughout Asia for its might and wealth.

Hampi has also been a pilgrimage centre from pre-Vijayanagara, Vijayanagara, and post-Vijayanagara times right down to the present. Besides its religious and mythological associations, the site is famous today for the magnificent ruins, both religious and secular, of the once fabled capital city. The term 'Hampi' is used in this book not just to mean the present-day village near the Virupaksha temple complex, but the site of the medieval Vijayanagara city which extends far beyond it.

In the past, Hampi was rather inaccessible; and if reaching it was difficult, travelling around the ruins was somewhat an adventure:

the bullock-cart was the sole means of transport available locally even about thirty years ago! In the last decade or two, however, Hampi has been opened to visitors from India and abroad. The nearest town, Hospet, thirteen kilometres away, is linked by road and rail to the principal cities of the country. When I first visited the site in the early 1980s, the only suitable accommodation available for a visitor in the site proper was the two-bedroom PWD Inspection Bungalow at Kamalapuram. Recently, a number of lodges and guest-houses have opened in Hampi and there is also a three-star hotel at Kamalapuram. Bicycles, autorickshaws, and tourist taxis are easily available on hire. A tourist bus service is also provided for the visitor who wishes to cover the site in a single day.

'The City of Bidjanagar [Vijayanagara] is such that the pupil of the eye has never seen a place like, and the ear of intelligence has never been informed that there existed anything to equal it in the world', remarked Abdur Razzak, an envoy from Herat to the court of Devaraya II in 1443. The city is situated amidst very impressive surroundings, the most striking feature of which is the river Tungabhadra that flows here in a north-easterly direction through a rugged, rocky terrain. The pinkish-grey granite boulders form fantastic shapes as though piled up by some mysterious spirit. To the south of the river are two ridges, separated by a valley, and low hills such as the Hemakuta and the Matanga. Immediately to the south of these, the landscape changes to open valleys with isolated rocky outcrops, such as the Malyavanta. Gradually, the hills disappear and the land becomes increasingly flat and open. The larger valleys are irrigated. The contrast between the stark rocks and green, fertile valleys adds to the picturesqueness of the site.

The remains of the city of Vijayanagara, popularly known as the 'Hampi ruins', are spread over an extensive area of about twenty-five square kilometres from the village of Hampi in the north to Kamalapuram in the south. The outer lines of its fortifications and the suburban areas, however, include a much larger area, from at least Anegondi in the north to modern Hospet in the south [Fig. I].

The city was called Hosapattana, the 'New City', for some time. Later it came to be known as Vijayanagara or 'City of Victory' and in the sixteenth century also as Vidyanagara or 'City of Learning'.

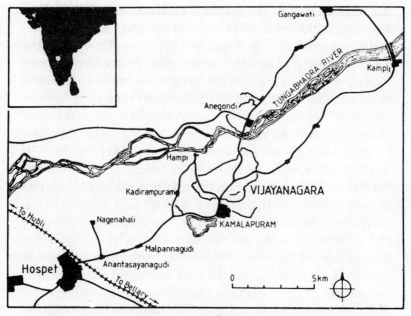

Fig. I. Vijayánagara in its regional context

Hampe, Pampa-kshetra, Pampa-pura are some of the other names by which the site is identified in epigraphs, though perhaps, these refer more particularly to the sacred area on the south bank of the river and not to the entire metropolis.

Besides the Persian traveller Abdur Razzak, other foreign travellers have also left glowing accounts of the splendours of Vijayanagara. These include the Italian Nicolo Conti in the early fifteenth century, his compatriot Varthema in the beginning of the sixteenth century, and the Portuguese Duarte Barbosa, Domingo Paes, and Fernao Nuniz also in the sixteenth century.

To facilitate documentation and for a convenient differentiation between the zones in this vast site, the entire area has been divided into four functional zones: the 'sacred centre', the 'intermediate irrigated valley', the 'urban core' and the 'suburban centres'.

The 'sacred centre' lies to the south of the Tungabhadra. Here, in the confined areas of flat land or at the summits of rocky outcrops, are located the largest temple complexes of the city, numerous smaller temples and shrines, sculptures, and inscriptions. To the south is the 'irrigated valley'. The paucity of buildings and potsherds here indicate that this was always an agricultural zone. The 'urban core' occupies a series of hills, ridges, and valleys to the south of the 'irrigated valley'. The greatest concentration of population was once located here, as is revealed by the traces of residences, tanks, wells, roads, stairways, pottery, and also the remains of many small shrines and larger temples. This zone is surrounded by a complete circuit of fortification walls, approximately oval-shaped, more than four kilometres along its southwest-northeast axis, broken only by well-defended gateways. In the southwest end of the 'urban core' is the 'royal centre' (also referred to as the 'palace zone'), which once had its own enclosure wall, only parts of which now survive. To the north, the 'urban core' is bounded by the north ridge. In the east end of the north ridge and the north-east valley is the Islamic quarter. Beyond the 'urban core' further south and west, as far as modern Hospet, are laid out the great residential suburbs, which include the modern villages of Kamalapuram, Kadirampuram, Anantashayanagudi, Malpannagudi, Nagenahali, and parts of Hospet town. A few isolated religious structures and other stray monuments in these are all that survive of the once populous 'suburban centres'.

This book deals in some detail with the city proper, which is taken to include the 'sacred centre', the 'irrigated valley' and the 'urban core'. The 'suburban centres' have been described only very briefly.

TWO

Historical Context

Pre-Vijayanagara Hampi

The founders of the Vijayanagara kingdom did not build their capital in an uninhabited desert land. The discovery of neoliths and hand-made pottery at the site proves that the history of the Hampi region dates back to the neolithic/chalcolithic times. The epigraphical evidence shows that this area was under the control of various dynasties that successively ruled Karnataka, including the early Western Chalukyas, the Later-Chalukyas, the Hoysalas, and the Kampli chiefs. One of the Kampli chiefs was Vira Kampiladeva, who built a temple at the site in the early fourteenth century.

The Mythic Associations

This site has had an unbroken tradition of sanctity since pre-Vijayanagara times. It is a place of pilgrimage hallowed by the goddess Pampa and her consort Virupaksha. The eponymous goddess Pampa is the local *devi* and the most ancient deity of the area. This is evident from the fact that the place (Hampi), the pilgrimage area (Pampa-kshetra), the river (Pampa, another name for the Tungabhadra), the lake (Pampa Sarovar), and even the principal male deity of the site (Pampapati, namely the 'Lord of Pampa', another name of Virupaksha) derive their names from her. It must be remembered that the letter 'P' in old Kannada is often replaced by 'H' in modern Kannada. The worship of this goddess appears to be anterior to the seventh century AD, from when there are epigraphical references to 'Pampa'.

This local folk goddess came to be 'Sanskritized' in the pre-Vijayanagara period by being wedded to Virupaksha, a form of Shiva. Marriage with Shiva or one of his incarnations was an almost universal method in south India by which local goddesses were absorbed into the brahmanical pantheon. As a result, Pampa came to be considered as an incarnation of the goddess Parvati. The story of Pampa and Virupaksha follows the typical pattern of the south Indian *sthalapuranas* (texts that recount the mythic origin and traditions of a sacred spot), the central element of which is the myth of the devi's marriage to the god. Most of these sthalapuranas adhere to the classical Shaiva mythology in which the goddess goes through severe penances as a means of winning Shiva for her husband. In the tale, the gods send Kama-deva to wound Shiva with arrows of passion. An important variation in these tales is that the goddess is recounted as having performed her austerities in a particular local spot, instead of in the Himalayas. Thus, according to the sthalapurana of Hampi, Pampa is described as the 'mind-born' daughter of Brahma, who performed her austerities at Pampa Sarovar and as a result won over Shiva, who was seated in meditation on mount Hemakuta. The most important annual festivals in the Virupaksha temple to this day are the *Phalapuja* (betrothal) and the *Kalyanotsava* (marriage-festival).

As a result of this process of 'Sanskritization', the goddess lost in importance to the male deity. Indeed, the literary and epigraphical evidence indicates that by the twelfth century AD Virupaksha had already emerged as the principal divinity of Hampi. The Virupaksha cult gained greatly in importance with the founding of the Vijayanagara kingdom, with its capital built in the proximity of a temple dedicated to him. Virupaksha remained the presiding deity of Hampi during the Vijayanagara period and continues to be so till this day.

Besides being the seat of Pampa and Virupaksha, Hampi and its environs have also been closely associated with the *Ramayana*, for the site is believed to be the Kishkindha of the epic, the mythical monkey kingdom of Vali and Sugriva. The events of the *Ramayana* related to this site centre around the meeting of Rama with Hanuman and Sugriva and the alliance formed between them. When Rama's wife Sita was abducted by the demon king Ravana, Rama and his brother Lakshmana began searching for her. Travelling southwards, they reached the banks of lake Pampa, where they visited the hermitage of the female ascetic Shabari. In the meantime, Sugriva, the exiled monkey prince, and Hanuman, who had taken shelter at Rishyamuka, had witnessed Sita being carried southwards by Ravana in his aerial chariot. Seeing them, the desperate Sita had dropped her ornaments, tied in a scarf, hoping that these would guide her husband to her.

When Rama and Lakshmana approached Rishyamuka, Sugriva fled, suspecting them to be emissaries of his rival Vali. Hanuman, who met the two brothers, however, realized that they were friends and effected an alliance between Sugriva and the two strangers. Soon after this, Rama killed Vali, and Sugriva was enthroned as the king of Kishkindha. Then, during the rainy season, Rama and Lakshmana took shelter on mount Malyavanta. After the monsoons, on being reminded by Lakshmana of his promise of assistance to Rama, Sugriva sent his monkey cohorts in all directions in search of Sita. Hanuman and his band, who went south, returned with the news that Sita was in Lanka. On hearing this, Rama and Lakshmana, along with the monkey army, proceeded southwards for the epic battle against Ravana.

The places mentioned in the above account of the *Ramayana* are believed to be located in and around Hampi. Kishkindha is said to be in the hills that surround Anegondi. Anjenadri Hill, to the northwest of Anegondi, is the reputed birth-place of Hanuman or Anjaneya. Lake Pampa is situated near the foot of this hill. Close to it is the cavern thought to be Shabari's dwelling. The Rishyamuka hill is located on a large island to the north of the Matanga. A small cave amidst the boulders on the south bank of the river is known as Sugriva's cave, where the latter is said to have hidden Sita's jewels. Certain streaks in the sheet-rock closeby are believed to have been caused by Sita's scarf. Nearby is Sita Sarovar, where Sita is believed to have bathed and done penance after her subsequent abandonment by her husband. Rama is said to have given Sugriva a garland to wear at Chintamani, in Anegondi, in order to distinguish him from his brother Vali during their deadly combat that took place on a near-by rocky island in the river. A huge mound of scoriaceous ash in the village of Nimbapuram on the south bank is claimed to be the cremated remains of Vali. Lakshmana is said to have crowned Sugriva king at the site of the Kodandarama temple, also on the south bank.

The Malyavanta Hill, where Rama and Lakshmana were supposed to have waited, is crowned by the large Raghunatha temple. Madhuvana, where Hanuman and his companions descended to celebrate their success in discovering Sita before reporting the happy tidings to Rama, is identified at a place on the Hospet–Kamalapuram–Kampli road, about one and a half kilometres beyond the circuit wall of the 'urban core'.

A Brief History of the Vijayanagara Kingdom

The Vijayanagara state was founded in the mid-fourteenth century by two local princes, Hukka and Bukka, sons of Sangama. The earlier Hindu kingdoms of south India and the Deccan had been swept away by the overpowering might of the Delhi Sultanate in the early fourteenth century. However, the control of the latter over the territories south of the Vindhya mountains lasted only very briefly. Successful revolts resulted in the emergence of the Vijayanagara kingdom, around 1336, and of the Bahmani Sultanate in the upper Deccan in 1347, with its capital at Gulbarga, and later at Bidar. The Vijayanagara state established a new political and moral order based on traditional Hindu cultural values. It was a powerful military polity whose rulers, for more than 200 years, fought to attain supremacy in the Deccan and south India by warring against the rival Muslim sultans and other Hindu kings.

The choice of Hampi as their seat of power by the founders of this kingdom was not accidental. The strategic location of the site and military considerations influenced their decision. The Tungabhadra river afforded a natural protection on the north and the west, while the dramatic landscape of hillocks and rocky outcrops created a vast natural fortress. The rugged topography was ingeniously exploited by the rulers to defend the city and was soon woven into the system of fortifications that surrounded it. That it survived for more than 200 years on the edge of a territory heatedly disputed with the Bahmani sultanate and its successor states is a measure of the city's strength. Despite the fact that Vijayanagara was besieged a number of times, it was never stormed. Indeed, only when it was left undefended by the ruling elite, following the disastrous battle of 1565, was the city captured and sacked.

Besides the obvious natural advantages, the founders were also influenced in their choice of location by the site's mythic associations. The sons of Sangama, staunch Shaivas, were evidently devotees of the god Virupaksha and they decided to situate their power centre under his protection. Virupaksha was adopted as the patron deity of the kings, their capital, and the kingdom as long as Vijayanagara remained the capital, not only by the Shaiva Sangamas but also by the later dynasties which were Vaishnava in affiliation. The name of the guardian deity was adopted by these rulers as their insignia and royal epigraphs often end with 'Shri Virupaksha', which took the place of the signature of the king.

While invoking the protection of the local god Virupaksha, the rulers were also aware of the site's association with the *Ramayana*, which added partly to its auspiciousness. From the early fifteenth century onwards, when the Ramachandra temple was built in the heart of the 'royal centre', the *Ramayana* tradition at the site began to be greatly developed. In Indian tradition, Rama is considered to be the ideal king and at Vijayanagara, a deliberate homology came to be drawn between Rama, the ideal, universal monarch, and his earthly counterpart, the king reigning from Vijayanagara. This was achieved by highlighting Rama's movements through the sacred landscape in and around Hampi and through it's architecture and sculpture. The city was even compared to Ayodhya, Rama's capital. An inscription of 1379, for example, states, 'In the same city (Vijaya) did Harihara dwell, as in former times Rama dwelt in the midst of the city of Ayodhya.'

That this was believed to be a site under divine or cosmic protection is hinted at in various foundation myths. The most popular of them is the story of the 'Hare and the Hounds'. According to this tale, once Hukka and Bukka, the first two kings of Vijayanagara, were out hunting in the Hampi region when the hare that was being pursued by their hunting dogs suddenly turned on its adversaries and began to chase the fierce hounds. On being consulted by the two brothers, the great sage Vidyaranya, who was meditating at the site, explained the meaning of this omen—this was an auspicious spot to situate a capital for here the weak would become strong and would challenge the mighty. The *Rayavachakamu*, a Telugu text supposedly written at the court of Krishnadevaraya, emphasizes the same theme through a different myth. According to this seventeenth-century work, the Matanga Hill was the abode of the powerful sage Matanga, who had cursed Vali for having once polluted his hermitage. When Sugriva fled Kishkindha, fearing the wrathful vengeance of Vali, he took shelter on the Matanga Hill since he knew Vali would never dare to come near it. From this hill, which dominates the site, the power and protection of sage Matanga emanated outwards and it later extended to envelop the royal capital founded here by the Sangamas.

Three dynasties ruled from Vijayanagara: the Sangama (1336–1485), the Saluva (1485–1505) and the Tuluva (1505–65). **Hukka,** or **Harihara I** (1336–56), was succeeded by his brother **Bukka I** (1356–77) during whose reign the endemic Vijayanagara–Bahmani war began. Bukka's son and successor, **Harihara II** (1377–1404), was the first ruler of this line to assume the imperial title of *maharajadhiraja* ('King of Kings'). The most capable of the Sangama rulers were **Devaraya I** (1406–22) and **Devaraya II** (1424–46). After the latter, the kingdom declined under the weak rule of **Mallikarjuna** (1446–65) and **Virupaksha II** (1465–185). The debility of these kings facilitated the rise of a provincial governor, **Saluva Narasimha,** who usurped the throne. He tried to revive the prestige of the Vijayanagara state by reconquering lost territories.

He was succeeded by two minor sons, **Timma** (1491) and **Immadi Narasimha** (1491–1505), for whom the Tuluva minister **Narasa Nayaka** and later his son **Vira Narasimha** acted as regents. Vira seized the throne in 1505 and founded the third dynasty to rule Vijayanagara. He was succeeded by his half-brother **Krishnadevaraya** (1509–29), the most illustrious of the Vijayanagara sovereigns, who excelled in all his military ventures as well as in the patronage of religion, art, and culture. Krishnadevaraya was followed by his half-brother **Achyutaraya** (1529–42). In the power struggle following the latter's death, **Ramaraya**, son-in-law of Krishnadevaraya, triumphed and became the regent of **Sadashiva**, nephew of the previous monarch; and the *de facto* ruler.

To further his interests, Ramaraya entangled himself in the interstate rivalries between the Deccan sultanates, the most important of which, from Vijayanagara's point of view, were Bijapur and Golconda, which had been formed on the disintegration of the Bahmani kingdom at the end of the fifteenth and early sixteenth centuries [**Fig. II**]. After a series of alliances and wars, Vijayanagara regained the territory that it had lost after Krishnadevaraya, and even extended its limits. In the long run, however, Ramaraya's policy proved disastrous. The Deccan sultans, alarmed at the growing power of Vijayanagara, temporarily buried their differences, and in a joint action defeated Ramaraya and the Vijayanagara armies in the battle of Talikota, on January 1565. Following this defeat, the capital was occupied and looted. The Vijayanagara state never fully recovered from this catastrophe. The northern parts of its erstwhile territory came to be occupied by its enemies and Vijayanagara ceased to be an imperial capital. The truncated kingdom lingered on in the south under the kings of the Aravidu dynasty, with their capital first at Penukonda, then at Chandragiri, and finally at Vellore, while their feudatories, such as at Madurai, Thanjavur, and Gingee, gradually became independent.

The Vijayanagara rulers fostered the development of intellectual pursuits and the arts such as music and dance, literature, architecture, sculpture, and painting. They introduced new techniques in warfare, building, waterworks, and agriculture. They were also great patrons of religion. In the capital, it was not only the cult of Virupaksha that

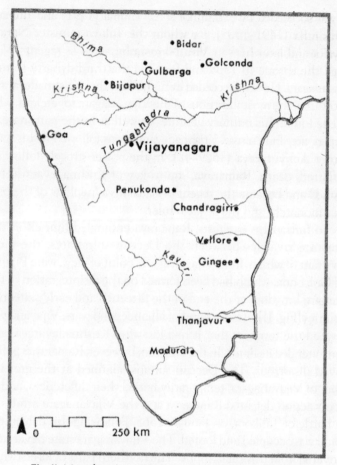

Fig. II. Map showing Vijayanagara on the Tungabhadra, with the Muslim capitals to its north and the later Hindu capitals to its south

received a great boost, the worship of Shaiva deities such as Mallikarjuna, Ganesha, and the fierce Virabhadra and Bhairava also became popular. The Vaishnava cult of Rama was greatly encouraged from the fifteenth century onwards. In the late fifteenth and sixteenth centuries, Vaishnava deities such as Krishna, Vitthala of Pandharpur, Tiruvengalanatha or Venkateshvara of Tirupati, and Ranganatha of Srirangam, were incorporated into the pantheon and the worship of minor divinities such as the *alvars* and *acharyas*, the saints of the Shri-Vaishnava sect, also gained recognition. While fostering and patronizing different Hindu sects and religious cults, the kings also permitted and even patronized the practice of other religions, such as Jainism and Islam, in the capital.

Inscriptions reveal that the Vijayanagara *rayas* and their subordinates gave lavish gifts to ascetics and sectarian leaders as well as to religious establishments. Hundreds of new shrines and temples were built in the capital and throughout the kingdom, while many old ones were repaired or extensive additions were made to them. Both religious men and temples were richly endowed with lands, money, taxes due to the state, jewels for daily worship, and even the institution of new festivals. The celebration of public rituals was an important function; for it was believed that flourishing festivals would strengthen *dharma*, establish the presence of divine powers in the kingdom, and stimulate the cosmic flow of gifts and fertility. The most important of these rituals preserving the cosmic order was, undoubtedly, the annual nine-day *Mahanavami* festival which culminated on the tenth day of *Vijayadashami* or *Dassera*. Domingo Paes, who visited Vijayanagara during the reign of Krishnadevaraya, has left a vivid account of this festival, a careful perusal of which makes clear that the festival, although basically religious in character, had political, economic, social, and military significance. The focus of the ceremonies was upon the reigning monarch and the revitalization of his realm. The various rites of this festival reveal that the king and the deity being worshipped were at least homologous, if not equal.

The patronage of religion, especially the royal celebration of public rituals such as Mahanavami in the capital, highlights the fact that in the Vijayanagara system the relationship between the king and god was one of partnership. The transactions between kings, temple deities, priests, and sectarian leaders point to a relationship of mutual interdependence. The priests made offerings to and performed services for the gods; the deities preserved the king, his kingdom and his subjects; and the monarch protected and awarded material rewards to the temples, priests, and sectarian leaders. Thus, while the temples and sectarian leaders bestowed honours and blessings on the sovereign, the ruler in turn conferred on them protection and riches. Even though the kings were not thought of as gods, they manifested divinity and maintained divine order in the world. Prosperity, fertility, success in war, the right relationship between the castes, all resulted, ultimately, from royal activity.

Growth of the City and Its Destruction

Under the enlightened leadership of the rayas, Vijayanagara became a rich, cosmopolitan blend of different peoples with a wide variety of linguistic, ethnic, and religious backgrounds. The growth of Hampi from a small pilgrimage centre to a mighty metropolis, which, according to the European visitors, was larger than Rome, Paris, or Lisbon, was gradual.

Although popular tradition and some spurious inscriptions ascribe the foundation of the city to Harihara I and Vidyaranya, Vijayanagara became the capital only during the reign of Bukka I. Harihara I ruled from Anegondi on the north bank of the Tungabhadra, which Paes refers to as the 'old capital'. With the establishment of the Bahmani sultanate and the commencement of warfare between the two Deccan states, Bukka I thought it prudent to shift his seat south of the river. His records assert that Bukkaraya was 'on the throne of the new Vijayanagara' and that he 'built a splendid city, called the city of victory'. But, Bukka's city was rather small, comprising only the 'royal centre', whose fortifications were built at this time. Two inscriptions referring to gateways at the eastern end of the 'royal centre' cite them as being 'east of the city of Vijayangara of Shri Vira Bukkaraya'.

The attentions of Bukka, and his successor, were primarily directed towards the military threat of the Bahmanis, and so they concentrated more on constructing the fortifications of Vijayanagara, rather than the temples. The earliest dated temples at the site are from the reign of Harihara II, but none of them are royal foundations. They are widely scattered over the site: a Jaina temple, now-a-days called the Ganagitti temple, is situated near Kamalapuram; is a small Shiva temple just outside a gateway in the south-eastern end of the fortifications around the 'urban core', and two Shaiva temples

in the 'sacred centre', one on the south bank not far from Koti-
tirtha and the other on Hemakuta hill. Thus, under Harihara II
the capital was already a well-developed and large city, extending
from present-day Hampi to Kamalapuram. Epigraphical references
to two gateways of the walls around the 'urban core' indicate that
this line of fortifications was in existence during this period.

Under the later Sangamas, new temples were built, of which
the most important was the one in the 'royal centre' dedicated to
Ramachandra. New quarters were also developed in the city.
Devaraya II made it a conscious policy to welcome Muslims into
his army, especially as cavalrymen and archers. That the Islamic
quarter at the north-eastern end of the 'urban core' was already in
existence during this time is revealed by a mosque built there by
Ahmad Khan, an officer of this raya.

The Tuluvas added great suburbs to Vijayanagara. The greatest
expander of the city and also an architectural innovater was
Krishnadevaraya. He had the suburb of Krishnapura laid out around
the Krishna temple, which he commissioned in 1515. Three suburbs
were built south of Vijayanagara proper, named respectively after
his mother Nagaladevi (modern Nagenahali), his principal queen,
Tirumaladevi (part of modern Hospet), and prince Tirumala, his
heir-apparent (modern Anantashayanagudi). Krishnadevaraya
himself shifted his residence from the city-centre to the new suburban
area south of it. He visited the city proper for the celebration of
public rituals.

Under Achyutaraya two new suburbs were laid out: Achyutar-
ayapura developed around the great temple of Lord Tiruvengalanatha,
constructed by the king's brother-in-law in 1534, and Vardadevi-
ammana-pattana, named after his principal queen, near Kamalapuram,
of which only the so-called Pattabhirama temple survives.

The destruction of this rich and splendid city was sudden and
dramatic. Following the catastrophe at Talikota, Vijayanagara was
first looted by bands of robbers and then systematically plundered
by victorious Deccan armies that camped there for six months.
The huge quantities of charcoal, heat-cracked basements; and burnt
architectural pieces found during the archaeological excavations
prove that parts of the city were torched. Caesar Frederick, who

visited the site in 1567, however, wrote that the city was not fully destroyed in 1565, and an unsuccessful attempt was even made to restore it as the capital. No longer the setting of an imperial dynasty, the city soon fell into ruins. Later, treasure-seekers and vandals added to the despoilation of Vijayanagara, and the forces of nature completed the destruction begun by man.

Post-1565 Occupation of the Site

From 1565 to 1800, the area within which Hampi is located—the modern Bellary district—passed through various hands. The hold of the sultans of Bijapur and Golconda over this region, following their victory at Talikota, was tenuous and it came to be split into small principalities under chieftains known as the poligars. Later, the Mughal emperor Aurangzeb annexed these territories. Subsequently, it was dominated by the Marathas, and still later by Haidar Ali and Tipu Sultan of Mysore. Through all these changes, however, the poligars continued to hold local authority. After the partition of Tipu's territory in 1792, part of the district fell under the Nizam of Hyderabad. Further division occurred after Tipu's death in 1799, and the Nizam obtained the rest of it. The Nizam ceded both these portions and the adjoining area to the British in 1800. These ceded districts were added to the Madras Presidency, of which it remained a part till India's independence and the subsequent reorganization of states, when Bellary district became a part of Karnataka.

Very little is known about what happened at the site from 1565 to 1900. Some stray references are available of developments in the Vitthala and Virupaksha temples, the two most important monuments at the site, during these centuries. A passing reference, for instance, is made in the Mackenzie manuscripts to some damage caused to the Vitthala temple by some Muslims during the period when Anegondi was occupied by the Maratha chief Shahujee. Again, in *Architecture in Dharwar and Mysore*, by Meadows Taylor and James Fergusson (published in 1866), a reference is made to Tipu Sultan having caused damage by gunpowder to the big-pillared hall of the Vitthala temple. The Mackenzie manuscripts also refer to Tipu's followers carrying away some of the jewels and silver of the Virupaksha temple. The historical accuracy of these accounts is open to question, but they point to the possibility of further destruction the site may have witnessed after 1565.

While there is no evidence of worship having continued in the Vitthala temple after the abandonment of the site, there is ample proof that the great Virupaksha temple continued as a religious establishment. The Aravidu dynasty did not break off its ties with Virupaksha, the patron deity of the kingdom. A copper-plate inscription of the second king Shriranga II, dated 1576, mentions a grant made in the 'presence of Virupaksha of Pampa-kshetra'. The Telugu work *Ramarajiyamu* mentions the visit of Chinna Venkata, a grandson of Ramaraya, to the temple of Virupaksha; and also of the mid-or late-seventeenth-century benefactions of prince Timma, nephew of the last monarch Shriranga III, who is said to have rebuilt the tall eastern *gopura* of the temple and maintained the worship of Virupaksha.

That the Virupaksha temple continued to be a place of worship and pilgrimage in the eighteenth and nineteenth centuries, and that it enjoyed patronage, is proved by the following: the superstructure of the northern gopura was constructed in the eighteenth century by the chief of Kanakagiri, a place not far from Hampi. On stylistic grounds, the paintings on the ceiling of the *maharangamandapa* belong to the late-eighteenth or early-nineteenth century and the big eastern gopura, as it appears today, seems to be a reconstruction of the same period. It is also known that the northern gopura of the temple was repaired in 1837 by the British Collector of the district. That in the mid-nineteenth century the principal festival of the temple was attracting large numbers as noted by a British antiquarian who describes crowds as large as 100,000 in one year, 60,000 in another and 40,000 in the third, over a period of fifteen years.

Thus, even after it ceased to be a capital city, Hampi continued to be inhabited and served as a centre of pilgrimage.

THREE

Architectural and Art Context

This chapter briefly describes the special features of the Vijayanagara architecture and art in order to give a contextual framework to the study of the monuments at the site.

Architecture

The extant monuments at Vijayanagara consist mainly of religious, courtly, and military buildings.

The primary building material used in all the standing structures is the locally available granite, found abundantly on the surface in the form of rocks and boulders. This stone is of a fine grain quality, which makes for even cutting. The method of quarrying the granite to get stone slabs and sheets was by striking wooden pegs into the boulder at regular intervals, a few centimetres from one another, all along the lines along which the rock was to be split. Water was then poured over the boulder, causing the pegs to expand. Coupled with an application of some more pressure, this process split the rock neatly. One can observe boulders that have been split in this manner all over the site. The slab that was detached was then cut, with hammer and other hand-held implements, into the required shape and size, and even polished if needed into dressed stone slabs. The granite blocks used in the temple architecture and for the outer facing of walls and gateways were usually dressed, while rougher varieties were used for the courtly monuments which were heavily plastered over. Even if the outer faces of walls and structures were of dressed stone, the core of thick walls was filled with stone rubble, and brick work.

The superstructures of temples and gopuras were made of brick and mortar. The brick was probably made locally. Courtly buildings and domed structures were built of stone rubble in mortar. Fine plaster and stucco decorations embellished the brick and mortar work.

It is, mainly the stone structures that have survived. Those made of perishable material, especially wood, have disintegrated. Since the residential structures were largely made of such materials, none have survived, although traces of rubble walls around the residences can be seen even today. Even of palaces, only the stone basements, rubble walls and some brickwork are found. Evidently the rest was made of wood. The residences of the elite sections were probably embellished with finely executed plaster work, metal work, ivory, cloth hangings, and mirror-work, all of which have long since disappeared.

Religious Architecture

As far as the religious architecture is concerned, there are Hindu and Jaina temples, and Muslim mosques, tombs, and gravestones at the site.

While the bulk of the Hindu temples at Hampi belong to the Vijayanagara period, a small portion may be assigned to the pre-Vijayanagara times. These are mostly located at the original pilgrimage centre on the Hemakuta hill and in and around the Virupaksha temple complex. The earliest of these are two temples from the ninth–tenth centuries, in the Rashtrakuta style. Of these, the best example is the Durgadevi shrine to the north of the

Virupaksha temple. A few lathe-turned columns, elaborate door-frames, and ceilings made of schist in the Later-Chalukyan and Hoysala idiom have also survived in the Bhuvaneshvari and Pampa-devi shrines within the Virupaksha temple complex. Most of the pre-Vijayanagara temples, however, are made of granite and are in the local Deccan style, characterized by stepped pyramidal stone superstructures, overhanging eaves, and a plain outer wall, occasionally decorated with a horizontal band of geometric or scroll design in the middle. These temples are all fairly small.

Two distinct strains can be seen in the Vijayanagara style of temple art and architecture: the local Deccan tradition and the imported Tamil style. Though the fourteenth-century temples are all in the former mode, by the fifteenth century the Tamil tradition gained ground, for it satisfied the increasingly elaborate ritualistic needs better than did the Deccan type of temple which had fewer components and smaller dimensions. Thus, in the developed style of the Vijayanagara temple architecture, the material used (granite, with brick and plaster for the superstructure), the general plan, and the various auxiliary structures, including the gopura or towered gateway, are mainly in the Tamil tradition.

Around 350 shrines and temples still survive in the core area of the erstwhile city. A majority of them are small shrines, some are medium-sized temples, and a few large temple complexes. The former comprise only a sanctuary, or a cella and porch, or a cella, with a small mandapa and a porch. A medium-sized temple has a garbha-griha (sanctuary), a shukanasi (antechamber), an antarala (second antechamber), a rangamandapa (enclosed pillared hall, usually with four doorways), all arranged axially. Larger ones have, in addition to these, a closed circumambulatory passage around the sanctuary and an open mahamandapa in front. Such temples stand within one or more prakaras (courtyards). The auxiliary structures within the courtyard of large temple complexes include a separate shrine for the consort-goddess, the kalyana-mandapa, with a raised platform in the centre for the reception of the deity and his consort at the annual celebration of their marriage, colonnades that line the enclosure walls, a kitchen and store-rooms, a hundred-pillar hall used for performances, shrines of subsidiary deities or saints, towering gopuras and, outside the temple enclosure, a temple tank and a chariot-street, which is also lined with a colonnade on either side.

The temple pillars are decorative. The most characteristic type of column is the one in which the shaft is cut into three square blocks, usually with reliefs on each side, separated by octagonal and sixteen-sided blocks. The composite piers are a sixteenth century phenomenon. In these, the central shaft has either a rearing *yali* (mythical monster) or horse in front, with or without a rider, or a cluster of colonettes attached to it [Ph. 1].

Besides the numerous Hindu temples and shrines at the site, there are also at least six Jaina temples. These are all fairly small in size, relatively plain and are invariably in the Deccan style of architecture. The Jainas seemed to have employed a deliberate archaism in their religious architecture.

In the stone portions of Hindu and Jaina temples, mortar or other binding material was generally not used; but metal clamps may have been occasionally employed.

At Vijayanagara there are also the remains of a number of Muslim tombs, gravestones, and at least two mosques. While the tombs often have domes and arches, the mosques are built in the post-and-beam style, more typical of Hindu temple architecture.

Courtly Architecture

Alongside the religious monuments are found secular structures of different types from the same period. Among these are some that employ easily recognizable elements of Islamic architecture, such as arches, domes, and stucco decorations. The most important of these are the 'Lotus Mahal', 'Queen's Bath', 'Elephant Stables' and some watch-towers. A careful study shows that these buildings demonstrate an effective synthesis of different architectural styles. Despite the use of Islamic architectural elements, they are neither Islamic nor Hindu, but typically Vijayanagaran. This is a courtly style mainly reserved for buildings connected with the king, the court, and the army.

Although no palace structure has survived intact, recent excavations have exposed the basements of a number of courtly

Photo 1. Composite pillars, *mahamandapa* of the Vitthala temple

residences. These follow an almost uniform pattern of three or four 'U' shaped recessed platforms, set one on top of the other, with traces of residential rooms on the topmost level. Associated with court life were other platforms, such as the 'King's Audience Hall' and the 'Mahanavami Platform'.

Military Architecture

The city was fortified by circuits of defensive walls. According to Abdur Razzak, the Persian envoy, there were seven circles of fortifications, one within the other. Varthema, the Italian traveller, however, describes only three. The circuit wall that is still more or less intact is the one around the 'urban core', which rises to a height of about six metres. Wherever feasible, the fortifications follow the rocky ridges, taking advantage of the natural defences of the site. They are interrupted by substantial gateways that provided the city with security. These gateways were defended by barbicans that created enclosures with high stone-faced walls. Within the gateways or the enclosures there are often small shrines or images of deities such as Hanuman or Ganesha [Ph. 2]. The entrances to

Photo 2. Images on a boulder within a gateway

these enclosures are usually not aligned with the gateways, making it necessary to take one or more turns before one can pass through them.

Gateways, traces of pavement slabs and steps, and the alignment of temples or other structures indicate the existence and direction of roads. Many of the important roads led into the 'royal centre', converging on the open space in front of the Ramachandra temple. Other roads proceeded around the 'royal centre', linking the outlying settlements of the city with the 'sacred centre'.

For its regular supply of water, the city mostly depended on the monsoon rains. Great and small tanks were created with earthen dam walls to trap rain-water, and canals conducted water from these tanks all across the Vijayanagara site. Small dams diverted water from the Tungabhadra into channels that irrigated fields at quite a distance from the river. The hydraulic scheme that irrigates the valley today reuses portions of the original Vijayanagara irrigational system. Remains of a complex hydraulic system are also preserved in the 'royal centre' in the form of stone channels, drains, aqueducts, storage tanks, and wells.

Painting

The temples and palaces of the city were once decorated with vividly coloured paintings. They were executed either directly on plastered walls, pillars, and ceilings to become part of the permanent décor, or on large cotton cloths to be displayed temporarily on special occasions. Unfortunately, due to the fragile nature of both plaster and cloth, almost nothing of this pictorial heritage survives. Only in some of the temples or palace basements are faint traces of pigments or designs still visible; as for example in the kalyana-mandapa of the Vitthala temple.

The best example of painting at Hampi is on the ceiling of the maharangamandapa of the Virupaksha temple. Recent detailed studies of the costumes, headdresses, and weapons depicted in the painting however reveal that these panels can be of no earlier date than the late eighteenth century.

Sculpture

A vast quantity of sculpture was produced at Vijayanagara and a substantial amount of it is still extant. However, except for a few individual pieces, the majority of the sculptures are not of a very high quality. This can perhaps be explained by the fact that much of the work was executed on locally quarried granite. The texture of this material makes it prone to flaking and, therefore, there exists few well-finished sculptures with intricate detail work. Another factor could be the unusually large sculptural output in the relatively brief span of time in which Vijayanagara served as the capital.

Of the materials employed, the local granite is undoubtedly the most commonly used. The majority of the sculptures in granite were roughly executed. This, however, was not important as the sculptures and reliefs were generally covered with a thin layer of plaster, enabling the artists to conceal the unevenness of the stone and to improve on detail. Finally, they were painted in lively colours. Some reliefs and a small number of statues were made of grey-green schist, a material not found at the site and probably imported from the Gadag region. This material enabled the artists to display their virtuosity in the rendering of details of dress, headgear, and jewellery. Stucco was extensively used in the fashioning of human figures, animals and birds, and foliage motifs to decorate the parapets of mandapas, the superstructures of shrines, and the ascending storeys of gopuras. Most of the fragile plaster has been eroded by the elements. Even then, the remaining fragments reveal that this material provided an opportunity for the artists to lavish great care and attention in the rendering of minute details and variations in costumes and other motifs.

There is an astonishing variety in scale in the Vijayanagara sculpture. Monumental carvings like the Narasimha monolith and the gigantic *linga* near the Krishna temple contrast with minute, delicate friezes.

Sculptures are found both in natural settings and in architectural settings. Among the former are the sculptures on boulders, monoliths, and slabs. Taking advantage of the numerous boulders that dot the terrain, the Vijayanagara sculptors carved innumerable images, mostly sacred, on the rocks, sometimes in inaccessible locations. Later on, a shrine or temple was constructed around some of these. This was the case with the Malyavanta Raghunatha and the Kodandarama temples. Sometimes rudimentary thatch shelters were erected to protect such carvings on boulders, as indicated by holes on the boulders into which a wooden frame was fixed to support the thatched roof. This obsession with carving images on boulders extended to monolithic sculptures hewn out of rocks, and shrines were often built around these and worshipped. Sculpted slabs were set up in temple sanctuaries or in open air. Among these, besides images of deities, are the *naga* (snake) stones, placed either in temple compounds or under trees, and *sati* and hero stones. Architectural settings include balustrades, temple walls, ceilings, parapets, towers and, above all, columns and piers.

Vijayanagara sculpture is always full of vigour and expression. The imagination of the artists is unrivalled. New themes, patterns, and iconographic formulas appeared here for the first time in Indian art. New icons were created and themes of everyday life came to the fore, such as, soldiers on horseback, clowns, acrobats, wrestlers, dancers and musicians, animals, and birds.

Conclusion

The artistic movement at Vijayanagara had a vital regenerating power, thereby creating a new aesthetic which determined the direction of subsequent artistic activity in southern India. The innovations that occurred in architecture, sculpture, and painting in the capital influenced artistic development over a vast area under Vijayanagara and its successor states.

FOUR

Description of the Monuments

I t would be worthwhile to begin a visit to the monuments with a climb to the top of the Matanga Hill, the highest point at the site. The best time to do so is early in the morning, so that one can reach the top just in time to catch the sunrise. Although there are steps right up to the top, both from the western and eastern sides of the hill, it is preferable to take the more evenly spaced southern steps. To reach these, the best route is from the big Ganesha (*'Kadalekalu'* Ganesha) shrine, across the ridge that connects the Hemakuta and Matanga hills via the Shrimad Rajachandra Ashram complex. Another way of reaching these steps is to go to the end of the Hampi bazaar and then to follow the path southwards, skirting the Matanga hill. On the summit of the hill is a temple to Virabhadra, a fierce form of Shiva. One can climb on to the roof of this temple to see the surrounding panorama, which gives a breath-taking view of the entire site: To the north lies the Tungabhadra river; with the Rishyamuka hill on a midstream island, and on the north bank one can see, in the distance, the Anjenadri hill, crowned by a small temple. The Virupaksha temple and the Hemakuta hill group of monuments are discernible to the west. To the northeast is the

Vitthala temple; and to the east, directly at the foot of the Matanga, is the Tiruvengalanatha temple complex. To the south, the enclosures and monuments of the 'royal centre' are faintly visible in the distance.

A word of caution—for security reasons it is not advisable to go up the Matanga hill alone; indeed, it is preferable to visit isolated monuments or to clamber around the rocks in company.

Another experience that is recommended is a ride in the river on a coracle (basket-boat) [Ph. 3]. This mode of transport was used in Vijayanagara times; the only difference being that while the Vijayanagara coracles were lined with hide, the modern ones are covered with a plastic sheeting. In those days horses and cattle, besides human beings, were ferried across on coracles. Today, bicycles and even the occassional motor-cycle can be seen on them! Coracles are available by the river to the north of the Virupaksha temple, at Chakra-tirtha, and also at Talarighat.

The site is so extensive there is no one fixed route for the visitor to follow [Fig. III]. Those who stay at the Hampi village would, naturally, prefer to begin their tour with a visit to the Virupaksha temple. After this, the visitor may choose one of two routes: the

Photo 3. A coracle in the Tungabhadra

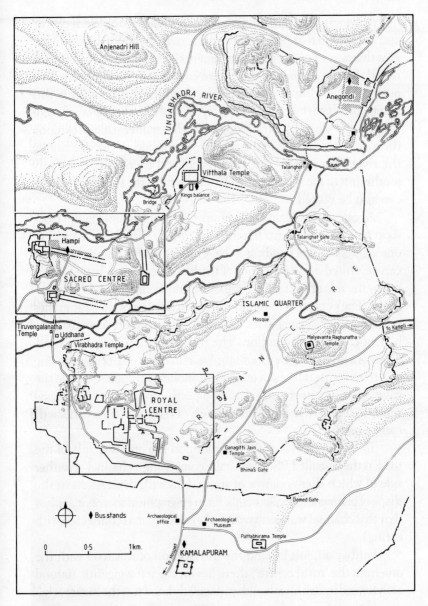

Fig. III. Map of Vijayanagara City

first that goes southwards from the Hampi village to the 'royal centre' and the second that proceeds along the river to the Vitthala temple. Another way of visiting the monuments is to follow a circular route round the site. This would be more convenient for those who are putting up at Hospet or at Kamalapuram. In this book, it is this latter route that is followed. Here it is proposed that the visitor proceeds towards the 'sacred centre' stopping at the smaller structures along the way. After the tour of the 'sacred centre', one can proceed along the river towards the Vitthala temple and then wind one's way southwards to the 'royal centre'. If time permits, the suburban centres can also be visited.

As one proceeds along the Hospet–Kamalapuram–Hampi road, soon after the road turns left into the 'royal centre', one notices to one's right a square building—the 'Queen's Bath'. This monument can be visited during the tour of the 'royal centre'. A little further on, by the side of the road are the Octagonal Fountain and 'Bhojana-shala'. The octagonal fountain is an open pavilion with large arches springing from square pillars. Originally this structure seems to have had much stucco decoration. The roof has a low octagonal dome. There is a deep octagonal fountain-basin in the centre of the building and to its south is found a massive monolithic trough. Outside the pavilion, remnants of earthen water-pipes that were used for supplying water to it and to the structures south of the road (now vanished) can be seen.

To the southwest of the pavilion, on the opposite side of the road, is the so-called Bhojana-shala, comprising a channel on either side of which there is a row of stone slabs with depressions in the shape of platters and shallow cups. From epigraphical sources it appears that this channel was known as *utada-kaluve* (canal connected with eating).

Further on, just beyond the intersection of this road with the one from the 'royal centre', there lies on the left a gigantic natural arch formed by two huge boulders, popularly known as the 'sister rocks'.

In the following description of the monuments, the exact dates mentioned are based on epigraphical evidences. When only an approximate date is cited, it is done on stylistic grounds.

Uddana Virabhadra temple

About half a kilometre north of the 'sister rocks' is one of the few temples where worship is still carried on. The priests here belong to the Virashaiva (Lingayat sect). The Virabhadra image within is 3.6 m high. The deity holds a bow and an arrow, a sword and a shield. A small figure of Daksha, with a ram's head, stands on one side. 'Uddana' means 'tall' in the local Kannada language. The inscription within the temple reveals that the deity was originally known as Mudu Viranna (i.e., 'sweet Virabhadra') and that this image was installed in 1545 by a Virashaiva general connected with the court. A unique prismatic linga is to be seen in the antechamber of the temple. The Mudu Viranna temple must have once been associated with the large monastic complex or feeding house for the brahmins, now in a dilapidated condition, within the banana plantation to the west of the temple.

Tiruvengalanatha temple of 1545

To the north of the Virabhadra temple lies this east-facing monument, termed Chandikeshvara temple. Its foundational inscription on a stone slab within, however, reveals that it was dedicated to the Vaishnava deity Tiruvengalanatha. It was consecrated in the same year as its neighbour and was donated by the same patron. The mandapa of this Vaishnava temple has elaborately carved yali columns. This hall provides access to two small shrines. A colonnade runs around them.

The Turuttu Canal flows near these two temples. In the Vijayanagara period, it was known as 'Hiriya-kaluve' (or 'big canal'). Just east of the main road, on the path alongside the canal, is the so-called Sarasvati temple, which was perhaps originally dedicated to Krishna. Traces of plasterwork suggest the rich decoration that once covered this apparently simple structure. A relief carved on a boulder a short distance to the east depicts a two-armed seated goddess, holding a ball of rice and a ladle. Though locally identified as the goddess Sarasvati, she is actually Annapurna, the goddess of food.

Monuments in the 'Sacred Centre', Along the Tungabhadra and in the 'Urban Core' (excluding the 'royal centre') [**Fig. IV**]

Monolithic Narasimha Image and Linga Shrine

A little to the north lies what remains of an imposing sculpture of Lakshmi-Narasimha. Narasimha, the man-lion divinity, an incarnation of Vishnu, is seated in a yogic posture on the coils of the cosmic serpent Sesha. Rising over the head of the deity is a multi-headed cobra hood surmounted by a yali, which forms part of an arch supported on two free-standing columns. There used to be a diminutive figure of the goddess Lakshmi positioned on Narasimha's lap. This monolith, 6.7 metres high, is the largest image at Vijayanagara. It was commisioned by Krishnadevaraya in 1528. This badly mutilated statue stands within an open structure with an entrance doorway on the east [**Ph. 4**].

Immediately to the north of the Lakshmi–Narasimha monolith is a square shrine that contains a giant polished linga, about 3 metres high. Due to recent irrigation in the vicinity, the base of the linga now stands in water.

Krishna Temple [see **Ph. B**]

This temple is one of the largest in the city. It was built in 1515 to house the image of an infant Krishna that Krishnadevaraya brought back as a war-trophy from Udayagiri after his successful capture of that hill-fort from the ruler of Orissa. This temple has two prakaras, each surrounded by high enclosure walls [**Fig. 5**].

Within the inner courtyard lies the main shrine and various subsidiary structures. The east-facing principal shrine consists of a garbha-griha, two antechambers, an enclosed circumambulatory passage, a rangamandapa with porches on the north and south sides, and an open mahamandapa with a four-pillar porch-like projection in front. To the northwest of the principal temple is a subsidiary shrine comprising an east-facing sanctuary and antechamber, a

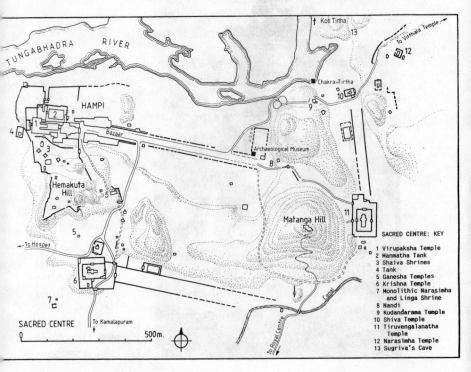

Fig. IV. Map of the 'Sacred Centre'

mandapa and a small south-facing sanctum opening on to the
mandapa. There are four other small shrines, one each in the north-
east and south-east corners and two in the south-west. Round the
enclosure wall is a pillared gallery. In the north-east and south-east
corners of this gallery are enclosed mandapas that probably served
as store-rooms or kitchens. There is a gopura in the middle of the
east, north, and south walls. The east gopura, though dilapidated,
is a majestic structure. On the west side of its superstructure is an
interesting depiction in stucco of troops in battle formation,
probably a scene from the Udayagiri campaign.

Photo 4. Monolithic
Narasimha Image

The outer irregular-shaped prakara has simple columned gateways, without superstructures, on the north, south, and east sides. In the north-west corner of this courtyard is a sixteen-pillar open mandapa and a small tank. On the south-west side is a unique six-domed structure, the only one of its kind in a Vijayanagara temple. This building has a small entrance on its eastern side with steps ascending to the roof. The absence of openings in the structure suggests that this was some sort of a storehouse, perhaps a granary. On the eastern side of the outer courtyard are some small pavilions.

To the east of the outer prakara is a long chariot-street, now under cultivation. Colonnades line this street, to one side of which is a large temple tank.

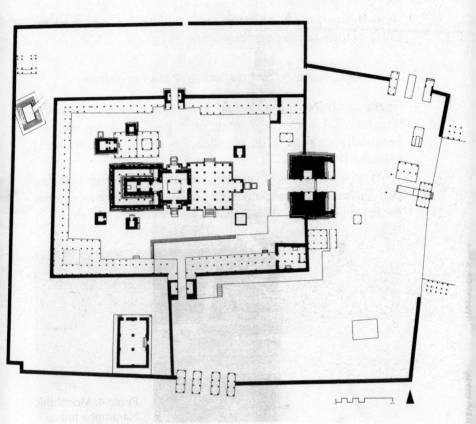

Fig. V. Plan, Krishna Temple Complex

The foundation of this temple and Krishnadevaraya's benefactions to it are recorded on a stone slab in front of the principal shrine and on the walls of the north-east sub-shrine. These inscriptions mention not only the construction of the temple but also the king's munificent gifts and endowments to it—valuable ornaments, gold and silver articles for the rituals, eleven villages to meet the expenses of different offerings and festivals and additional land for the maintenance of the thirty-seven brahmins appointed for various services in the temple.

Proceeding northwards along the road to the Hampi village, a medium-sized temple, dedicated to Narasimha, can be noticed just north of the Krishna temple complex.

Monolithic Ganesha Images and structures near them

To the northwest of the Krishna temple is a monolithic Ganesha sculpture, 2.4 metres high, in an open pavilion. Ironically, this beautifully sculpted image is called 'Sasivekalu' (mustard-seed) Ganesha [Ph. 5].

To the south of the Ganesha image is a small shrine, probably post-Vijayanagara, built around a carving of a pair of foot-prints encircled by a snake. Although one author has referred to this as

Photo 5.
'Sasivekalu'
Ganesha

Vishnupada, that is, the 'feet of Vishnu', it is more likely to be a representation of a Shaivite deity, probably Bhairava.

At the top of the ridge, before the road descends down to the Hampi village, is a temple that has an open pavilion with unusually tall, slender, and well-sculpted columns. The walls of the shrine are unadorned and its interior is dominated by an enormous monolithic image of Ganesha, more than 4.5 metres high. This image is referred to as 'Kadalekalu' (gram) Ganesha among the locals.

There is a gateway immediately to the south-east of this Ganesha shrine built across the road that originally led down to Hampi. This gateway is an open, columned structure with three passageways.

A path leads down to the Virupaksha temple's main gopura from behind this Ganesha shrine. The small, east-facing temple, with a columned gateway in front, is dedicated to Harihara, a composite deity, half Shiva and half Vishnu.

Proceeding along the pathway one arrives at the main entrance, facing east, of the Hemakuta group of temples.

Temples on Hemakuta Hill

The sacred Hemakuta Hill rises south of the village of Hampi. It is encircled by massive fortifications on three sides and is bounded on the north by the enclosure wall of the Virupaksha temple complex and by a colonnade, now mostly collapsed. Hemakuta is commanded by four gateways, two of which consist of open, double-storeyed colonnades. Of these, one is lower down the hill to the north and the other is at the summit of the hill to the south. These probably date to the mid-fourteenth century, immediately after the foundation of the capital, as do the fortification walls. A single-storeyed gateway is set into the walls at the southeast corner of the hill. Traces of rock-cut steps linking these gateways indicate a path that once led down to the river from the summit of the hill. This route was cut off by the sixteenth century enclosure walls of the Virupaksha temple. The principal entrance was an impressive gateway located near the bottom of the fortifications on the east side and perhaps dating from the fifteenth century.

There are more than thirty shrines on the Hemakuta hill, along with pavilions and water cisterns. The temples date from the pre-Vijayanagara and early Vijayangara periods. All were probably Shaiva in affiliation. They range from elaborate structures with multiple sanctuaries to small single-celled constructions. Two of the largest temples on the lower slope face northwards. They are similar in plan and elevation, each having three sanctuaries opening on to a columned hall that projects forward to form a porch with an over-hanging eave. Both temples have plain interiors. Their exteriors are characterized by sharply-moulded basements and plain wall surfaces with horizontal ornamented bands, while pyramidal stone superstructures, capped by a dome-like roof, rise over the sanctuaries. Part-circular projections extend from the front of the pyramidal towers. In the western temple, there is an inscription recording the installation of three lingas by Vira Kampiladeva, a local, early fourteenth-century chief. This epigraph suggests that the two temples were built in the decades immediately preceding the foundation of the Vijayanagara kingdom.

To the north-west of these two temples is another triple-shrine temple, facing east. It is the most ornate of the temples on the Hemakuta. To its north-east is a well-finished double-shrine temple.

The temples on the upper slope of the hill are less finely built. Among these is one that is locally known as the 'Mula' (original) Virupaksha temple. A large Hanuman image is installed in a shrine near it. Two inscriptions of 1398, one on the sheet-rock near the Mula Virupaksha temple, and the other on the vertical face of nearby cistern, refers to the construction of a temple dedicated to Virupaksha by two brahmin brothers. This temple is believed to be the east-facing temple near the cistern, comprising an open mandapa, an antechamber, and a sanctum.

Virupaksha Temple Complex

The Virupaksha temple, which was the pre-eminent religious centre at the site during pre-Vijayanagara and Vijayanagara times, remains an important pilgrimage centre even today. Its festivals, especially the *kalyanotsava* that culminates in the chariot ceremonies, attracts large crowds [Fig. VI].

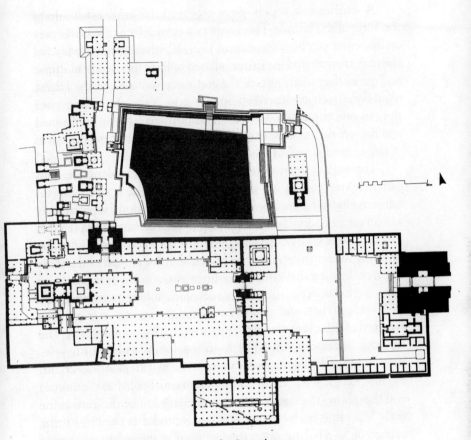

Fig. VI. Plan, Virupaksha Temple Complex

The Virupaksha temple can be entered from the east through a lofty gopura, an early nineteenth-century renovation of an earlier structure [see **Ph. A**]. Its diminishing brick and plaster storeys creates a pyramidal tower about fifty metres in height. Some fifteenth-century carved blocks are set into the stone base of this gateway, which gives access to the outer enclosure of the temple. In the south-west corner of this courtyard is the 'hundred-pillar' hall and in the north-west corner the kalyana-mandapa. A doorway in the south side of the hundred-pillar hall leads into a kitchen, a colonnaded structure with a water channel cut into its rocky floor.

A smaller east gopura gives access to the inner enclosure of the Virupaksha temple. This gateway was built by Krishnadevaraya on the occasion of his coronation in 1509–10, when he also constructed the maharangamandapa (front pillared hall) of the principal shrine and gave other costly gifts to the god Virupaksha. Records of these royal donations are inscribed on two stone slabs, the first to one's right as one enters the outer courtyard through the big east gopura and the second just in front of the maharangamandapa, to the north of the eastern steps of this structure [Ph. 6].

The walls of the inner enclosure are lined by a colonnade. This gallery houses various sub-shrines. The core of the temple, now totally enveloped by the Vijayanagara period additions, was probably a small shrine dating back to about the twelfth century. The principal shrine, that of god Virupaksha, as it appears today was built in the fifteenth-sixteenth century. The principal shrine comprises the sanctuary, enshrining the Virupaksha-linga, surrounded by an enclosed circumambulatory passage, a couple of antechambers, a rangamandapa with side porches, and an open maharangamandapa in front. The columns of this outer mandapa are carved with great virtuosity. The spacious interior is defined by sixteen columns with rearing yalis. The ceiling of this open central area is covered with paintings depicting mythological scenes, except for an unusual panel at the eastern end that shows the sage Vidyaranya (believed to be the guru of the early Vijayanagara monarchs and a co-founder of the city) being carried off in a palanquin in the company of musicians and drummers. The most important panels are arranged in matching pairs on either side of the central lotus: the marriage of Shiva and Parvati with the marriage of Rama and Sita, the ten incarnations of Vishnu with the eight guardian deities of the universe's directions, Shiva shooting an arrow at the demons of the three cities with Kama aiming an arrow at Shiva in meditation.

To the northwest of the principal shrine lie smaller shrines of the goddesses Pampa and Bhuvaneshvari, both identified as the consorts of Virupaksha. The interiors of these shrines are noteworthy for their schist pillars, ceilings, and doorways, carved in the typically ornate manner of the later Chalukyas. These appear to have been brought from elsewhere and reassembled here. A doorway to the

Photo 6. Principal shrine, Virupaksha Temple

west of the principal shrine leads to a shrine dedicated to the sage Vidyaranya. Besides the east gopura, the inner enclosure wall also has a north gopura. Its granite base is of the fifteenth century, while the brick and plaster superstructure was probably added in the eighteenth century.

Manmatha tank and overlooking shrines

The Manmatha tank lies to the north of the Virupaksha temple. Close to it are a number of small temples, mostly from the pre-Vijayanagara period. The most important in this group is the red sandstone Durgadevi temple dating back to the ninth or tenth century. A large eight-armed image of Durga is placed within its sanctuary. In its mandapa is a slab with an inscription that records a donation made by a local chief to Virupaksha in 1199. A sculpture of a warrior battling a lion is placed near it.

Hampi Bazaar

The ceremonial street for the chariot festivals stretches eastwards from the outer east gopura of the Virupaksha temple. It is locally known as the Hampi bazaar. It is more than ten metres wide and almost 750 metres long, lined for much of its length with raised colonnades and structures, some of which are double-storeyed. At its western end these colonnades and structures have been incorporated into newly built shops, restaurants and residences and some have even been pulled down. A large structure at the northeast end of the street has been converted into a museum by the Karnataka State Directorate of Archaeology and Museums. At the eastern end of the bazaar lies a large two-storeyed mandapa with some well-carved schist pillars of the later Chalukyan type. A pavilion to the northeast shelters a large monolithic image of Nandi. A stepped path from here leads over a ridge, through an open gateway, to the Tiruvengalanatha temple complex.

For visitors travelling in a vehicle, it is best suggested that the conveyance be sent to the Vitthala temple, and the monuments by the river be covered on foot.

Monuments at Chakra-tirtha

A path turning off to the north from the Hampi bazaar leads to the Tungabhadra river. This path provides a magnificent vista of the river, rocks, and hills. Chakra-tirtha, where the river takes a northerly bend, is an auspicious bathing spot. According to a local legend, it is hallowed as the place where Vishnu propitiated Shiva by his penances and received from him the magical weapon, the *chakra* (discus).

It is also believed that it was here that Lakshmana, Rama's brother, crowned the monkey king Sugriva. According to the local lore, this event took place where the north-facing Kodandarama temple stands today. This temple is still used for worship. Locals believe that Rama is the brother of goddess Pampa, and to this day certain rituals of the betrothal ceremonies of Pampa and Virupaksha are performed at this temple during the annual *phalapuja* festival. This temple has a sanctuary, built against a rock-carving of Rama, Lakshmana, Sita and Sugriva, and a mandapa with tall, sculpted columns.

There are a number of smaller shrines immediately to the south of the Kodandarama monument that are open only when the daily rituals are performed. The Yantroddharaka Anjaneya temple has a magnificent rock-carving of Hanuman in meditation inside a *yantra* (mystic diagram) of two intersecting equilateral triangles within a circle, the circumference of which is covered by a string of twelve jumping monkeys. In the so-called Surya-Narayana shrine, there is a brilliant image of the personified chakra *of* Vishnu. The small temple with a stepped pyramidal stone superstructure, situated on a high platform, locally known as the Hastagiri Ranganatha-svami temple, was originally dedicated to Vitthala, and it predates the great Vitthala temple complex. It is referred to in an epigraph as the Prata Vitthala temple.

To the east of the Kodandarama temple and at the end of the Tiruvengalanatha chariot-street stands a Shiva temple from the early Vijayanagara period. It is locally known as the Varaha temple because the boar emblem of the Vijayanagara rulers is carved on its gopura.

Photo 7. Miniature *lingas* at Koti-tirtha

Koti-tirtha

A walk by the side of the river from Chakra-tirtha to Koti-tirtha, a short distance away, is highly recommended. This spot contains a mass of rocks and boulders, which provided the Vijayanagara sculptors ample opportunity to demonstrate their skills. Here there are two rock-shelters with interesting Vaishnava reliefs. In the lower one, the twenty-four forms and ten incarnations of Vishnu, the episodes of the story of Narasimha, and the images of Vitthala and Venkateshvara are carved against the vertical surfaces of the rock. In the higher rock-shelter, which is difficult to reach, there are images of Rama, Sita, and Narasimha.

At Koti-tirtha, there are two groups of miniature lingas arranged symmetrically in a square design around a larger central linga [Ph. 7]. They are carved on the horizontal surface of the boulders. Among the other noteworthy carved figures are—Vishnu as Anantashayana, reclining on the cosmic serpent, two reliefs of Narasimha, one of Surya (the sun-god) and one of Parvati flanked by her sons, Ganesha, and Subrahmanya.

There are also two small temples at Koti-tirtha, built into the rocks, each with beautiful sculptures. In the smaller of the two is an elegantly executed relief of Parvati and some devotee figures. Along the passage leading to the larger of the two temples are carvings of the seated Bhairava and Bhairavi, Virabhadra with consort and standing Shiva in the form of Chandrashekhara. Within the temple are reliefs of Shiva as Dakshinamurti, the great teacher; Durga killing the buffalo demon Mahishasura; Surya on his chariot riding around the mythical mount Meru; and the panels of portrait sculptures with label inscriptions of Ramachandra Rayasta Dikshita and family. Unfortunately, some of these portrait carvings, the best examples of such sculptures at the site, were recently vandalised.

Tiruvengalanatha Temple Complex

The unusual northern orientation of this temple is explained in part by the course of the valley in which the temple and its long chariot-street are laid out. The valley is bounded by the Matanga

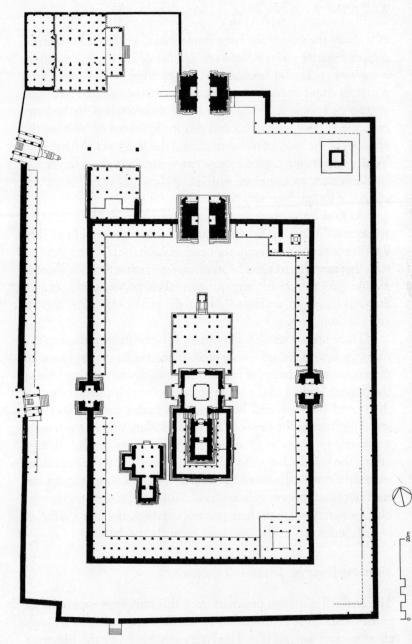

Fig. VII. Plan, Tiruvengalanatha Temple Complex

A. Virupakṣha Temple *gopura*, as seen from Hampi bazaar

B. Krishna Temple Complex

C. Ramachandra Temple

D. The octagonal watch-tower in the 'Zenana Enclosure', Madhava Temple and rocks

Hill to the west and the Gandhamadana Hill to the east. This temple is commonly known as the Achyutaraya temple, even though its patron is known to have been Hiriya Tirumala, the king's brother-in-law and chief minister. This is recorded in an epigraph inscribed on the inner northern gòpura, which records that the temple was consecrated in 1534 when an image of Vishnu as Tiruvengalanatha was enshrined in its sanctuary.

The Tiruvengalanatha temple complex [**Fig. VII; Ph. 8**] is one of the largest complexes in the city and the only one that has two complete rectangular courtyards, one within the other. In the inner enclosure is the principal shrine, with a sanctum, two ante-chambers, an enclosed circumambulatory passage, a rangamandapa, a mahamandapa and a small cell in front for Garuda, the *vahana* (vehicle) of Vishnu. The subsidiary shrine is to the southwest of the principal temple. Its mandapa has some unusual pillar-reliefs of courtly figures. There are three gopuras in the inner enclosure wall. In the north-west corner of the outer enclosure is a hundred-pillared hall, which has some exceptional pillar-reliefs. The outer enclosure has a large north gopura, two smaller gateways on the western side and a small opening to the south.

The south doorway leads to a path that winds round the base of the Matanga Hill into the irrigated valley. A boulder carved with a multi-armed image of Kali, now brightly painted, overlooks this path. Like other great temple complexes, the Tiruvengalanatha temple, too, has a long chariot-street and a temple tank.

Narasimha temple and Sugriva's cave

The small Narasimha temple, with a stepped pyramidal stone superstructure typical of the pre- and early-Vijayanagara temples, is the earliest structure still standing in this part of the site. Although there is no foundational inscription to help date this monument, an inscription found here of 1379, mentioning additions made to it in that year, indicates that it was in existence prior to that date. The temple has a plain exterior except for relief carvings of Garuda and Hanuman.

Between the Narasimha temple and the river is a mound of

Photo 8. Tiruvengalanath Temple Complex

high boulders within which there is a spot called Sugriva's cave, a deep cleft between two rocks. A shallow pond close by is known as Sita Sarovar.

Bridge and Mandapa

A little to the north are some granite pylons, the remains of a bridge that once connected the two banks of the Tungabhadra at a point where the river turns eastwards.

Nearby, on the river bank, is a mandapa now associated with Purandaradasa, the famous sixteenth century musician and Vaishnava devotee.

Gateway and 'King's Balance'

The path from the Narasimha shrine to the Vitthala temple passes by an overturned sati-stone, which stood upright till a few years ago when it was unearthed, evidently by treasure-seekers. Both sides of the path are littered with small mounds of stone, placed by pilgrims who believe that this act will ensure good fortune.

The path passes through an open two-storeyed gateway. Here there are a number of small shrines. Further down the path is an unusual feature locally called the 'King's Balance'. It comprises two columns and a lintel, in the middle of which is a stone loop, from which a balance or swing was once suspended. The path continues towards the southern gopura of the Vitthala temple, but before that there stands an incomplete gopura, with fine carvings on its basement and interior doorway jamb.

Vitthala Temple Complex and Adjacent Structures

The Vitthala temple [Fig. VIII; Ph. 9], the finest example of religious architecture at Vijayanagara, was dedicated to Vishnu in the form of Vitthala. It consists of a large rectangular courtyard bounded by high walls. The courtyard can be entered through three gateways. A colonnade, now collapsed, lines the inner face of the enclosure walls. In the middle of the courtyard stands the principal temple and to the northwest and southwest are the subsidiary shrines. There

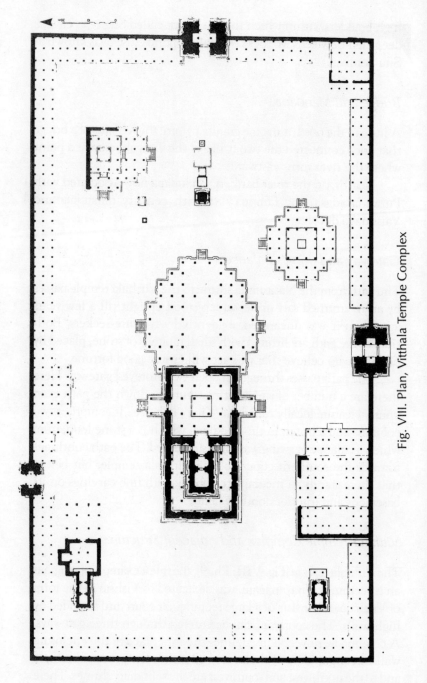

Fig. VIII. Plan, Vitthala Temple Complex

Photo 9. Principal shrine, Vitthala temple

are two free-standing mandapas in the northeast and southeast. A hundred-pillar hall is built into the south colonnade. A small shrine for Garuda, the eagle vehicle of Vishnu, fashioned in the form of a ceremonial chariot, stands in front of the principal temple. While the name of the original patron and the foundation date of the Vitthala temple are unknown, it is probable that the core of the principal shrine, the sanctum, the two antechambers, the enclosed circumambulatory passage around these, and the rangamandapa, were built prior to the sixteenth century.

There are over thirty inscriptions in and around the Vitthala temple, the largest number in any one temple in the city. These epigraphs indicate that substantial additions were made to the temple from 1513 to 1554, during the reigns of Krishnadevaraya, Achyutaraya, and Sadashiva. In 1513, the two queens of Krishnaraya, Chinna-devi and Tirumala-devi, donated the gopuras. The king himself commissioned the hundred-pillar hall in 1516. In 1534, the alvars were installed in a shrine to the north within the enclosure. In 1554 the magnificent 'swing pavilion', which is believed to be the open-columned hall of the principal shrine, was constructed by a chief closely connected with the court. This mandapa is elevated on an ornate basement, adorned with friezes depicting horses with attendants and miniature shrines housing images of the ten incarnations of Vishnu. It has fifty-six pillars, all of the composite variety. These include the so-called 'musical pillars', though, contrary to popular belief, the tones that are emitted when the colonettes of the pillars are lightly struck do not form part of a musical scale. The outer piers have groups of fluted colonettes clustered around central shafts. The central piers in the middle of each side have, in addition, fully modelled yalis. The distribution of the inner columns is varied so as to create open spaces on three sides of a central enlarged hall. Many of these columns are covered with figures and yalis, some sculpted almost in the round. The beams that span the central hall, where preserved, are more than ten metres long. The ceilings have elaborate lotus designs and other motifs. The outer columns are supported by a graceful, double-curved eave, ornamented with bands of foliation and upraised feather-like motifs at the corners. Stone rings here once supported lamp chains. Only portions of the brick parapet above survive.

Photo 10. Stone-chariot, Vitthala temple

The Garuda shrine, which is in the form of a stone-chariot, has four stone wheels, cut out of separate stone blocks. The stone-chariot originally had a brick and plaster superstructure, which was demolished in the nineteenth century [Ph. 10].

The southeast corner hall is popularly known as the kalyana-mandapa. It is laid out on a symmetrical plan with a raised platform in the centre. The basement, columns and ceiling of this mandapa are elegantly sculpted.

The Vitthala temple faces east and overlooks a chariot-street, about a kilometre long and forty metres wide. To the north of the ceremonial street is temple tank and at the end of it is an exquisite mandapa which served as the halting place for the temple chariots as they were drawn along the street.

The Vitthala temple [Fig. IX:1] was surrounded by four streets, through which the deity was carried in procession around the temple. Along these streets are a number of shrines and structures. Some of the shrines are dedicated to the Vaishnava saints. The temple to the northwest [Fig. IX:2] is that of Tirumangai-alvar; and the inscription on its eastern wall states that it was built in 1556. It is a fairly simple structure, except for the reliefs on its pillars and

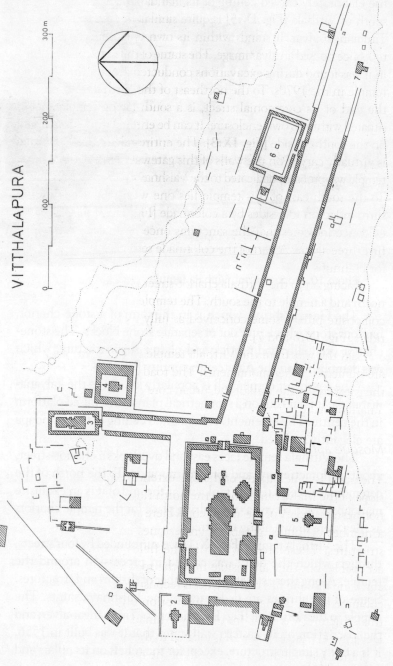

Fig. IX. Vitthalapura

the elaborately carved ceiling of its mandapa. The temple to the south of Vitthala [**Fig. IX:5**] is quite similar in plan to the one of Tirumangai-alvar. It stands within its own enclosure. Probably it, too, once housed an alvar image. The statue of the saint now installed in it was found during excavations conducted around the Vitthala temple in the 1970s. To the northeast of the Vitthala complex, at the end of its ceremonial street, is a south-facing temple that is situated within its own enclosure. It can be entered through a gopura on the southern side [**Fig. IX:3**]. The entire tale of the *Ramayana* is virtually carved on the walls of this gateway. This medium-sized temple was probably dedicated to the Vaishnava preceptor Ramanuja. To the south-east of this temple lies one with triple sanctuaries, surrounded on four sides by a colonnade [**Fig. IX:4**]. Inscriptional evidence indicates that the sanctums once housed images of the first three alvars. A part of the colonnade served as a feeding place for brahmins.

Facing on to the Vitthala chariot-street is a temple tank to the north and a temple to the south. The temple mandapa has a row of composite pillars, some conceived as fully modelled horses with riders [**Fig. IX:6** and **7**].

On the way from the Vitthala temple towards Kamalapuram are numerous other monuments. The road passes through one of the gateways in the wall of the 'urban core', now referred to as the Talarighat gate.

Mosque and tomb

The main Islamic quarter of the city extended from the northern slope of the Malyavanta hill to the north ridge, which marked the northern boundary of the 'urban core'. Here are found two mosques, a number of tombs, groups of gravestones and some columned structures. These are now within the fields and are not easily accessible, but they are visible from the road when the crops are cut. One mosque has recently been reconstructed. It consists of a columned hall, facing east. An inscription on a beam states that this structure was built in 1439 by Ahmad Khan, an officer of Devaraya II [**Ph. 11**]. A well is located to the north of the mosque. A domed tomb stands to the south of the monument.

Photo 11. Ahmad Khan's mosque and tomb

Malyavanta Raghunatha temple

This temple is located on the road to Kampli, which joins the Kamalapuram-Hospet roadway. Raghunatha is another name for Rama. This large temple stands on the summit of the Malyavanta hill. It has an enclosure wall with three gopuras. Within the courtyard is the principal temple, a subsidiary shrine, a hundred-pillar hall and some auxiliary structures. The sanctum of the main temple is built around a massive boulder which has carvings of the seated Rama and Sita accompanied by Lakshmana and Hanuman. The boulder protrudes from the top of the shrine and is also visible from the enclosed circumambulatory passage around the sanctum. On the enclosure wall are some large reliefs of serpents, fish, tortoises and other aquatic creatures. A small doorway on the west side of the enclosure wall gives access to a rocky shelf, from where one has a commanding view of the urban core. A crevice in the sheet-rock here is lined with rows of small low-relief Nandi images and Shiva lingas. This crevice is locally known as Lakshmana-bana for it is believed that it was here that Lakshmana shot an arrow into the earth and created the cleft from which water spouted forth.

Ganagitti Jaina temple

This is one of the earliest dated monuments at Vijayanagara [Ph. 12]. According to an inscription on the base of the lamp-column in front of it, this monument was erected in 1385 AD by a Jaina minister of Harihara II and was dedicated to the Jaina *tirthankara* (saviour) Kunthu Jinanatha. This north-facing temple is simple and unadorned. It consists of two connected mandapas, each with an adjoining square sanctuary. There are porches to the north and east.

Bhima's Gate

To the southeast of the Jaina temple is an impressive gateway that is popularly referred to as Bhima's Gate because of an image of the hero Bhima, from the Mahabharata, carved on a slab and also because of relief carvings of the episode of Bhima's killing of Dushasana.

Photo 12. Ganagitti Jaina Temple

Monuments of the 'Royal Centre' [**Fig. X**]

The first significant monument en route the 'royal centre' from Kamalapuram is the so-called 'Queen's Bath', a pleasure pavilion with balconies, overlooking a central square tank. Traces of its original plasterwork still survive. The structure is surrounded by a water channel [**Ph. 13** and **Fig. XI**].

A Shiva temple, locally known as the Chandrashekhara temple, is about 100 metres to the northeast. It stands within a rectangular walled courtyard, which can be entered from the east through a gopura. To the north of the Shiva temple is a small north-facing temple that stands on a boulder. Though locally believed to be dedicated to Sarasvati, inscriptional evidence reveals that it was a Tiruvengalanatha temple. To the northeast of this shrine is an octagonal arcade surrounding a tank in the centre of which is an octagonal platform. To the north of this octagonal bath, in a rocky outcrop, is a rock-cut shrine, comprising a small antechamber and a sanctuary. To the east of the octagonal bath and the shrine are a number of recently cleared ruined palace complexes.

Photo 13. 'Queen's Bath', interior

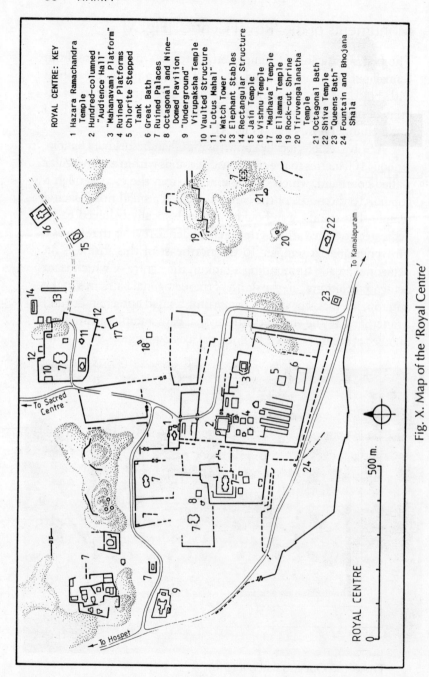

ROYAL CENTRE: KEY

1 Hazara Ramachandra Temple
2 Hundred-columned "Audience Hall"
3 "Mahanavami Platform"
4 Ruined Platforms
5 Chlorite Stepped Tank
6 Great Bath
7 Ruined Palaces
8 Octagonal and Nine-Domed Pavilion
9 "Underground" Virupaksha Temple
10 Vaulted Structure
11 "Lotus Mahal"
12 Watch Tower
13 Elephant Stables
14 Rectangular Structure
15 Jain Temple
16 Vishnu Temple
17 "Madhava" Temple
18 Ellamma Temple
19 Rock-cut Shrine
20 Tiruvengalanatha Temple
21 Octagonal Bath
22 Shiva Temple
23 "Queens Bath"
24 Fountain and Bhojana Shala

To Sacred Centre

To Hospet

To Kamalapuram

ROYAL CENTRE

500 m.

Fig. X. Map of the 'Royal Centre'

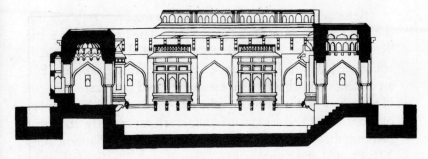

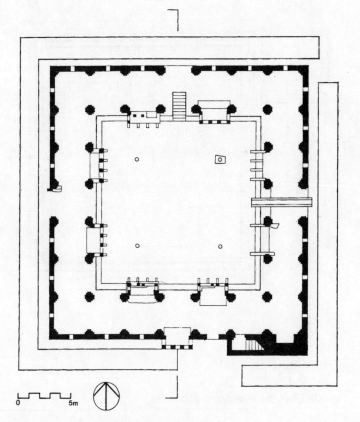

Fig. XI. Section and Plan, 'Queen's Bath'

Returning to the 'Queen's Bath', the road proceeds towards the various enclosures of the palace zone. The first of these is the 'Royal Enclosure' within which are found the high hundred-columned hall, which probably served as the King's Audience Hall, an underground chamber, an elegant stepped tank fashioned out of schist that was excavated in the mid-1980s, [Ph. 14] a number of other tanks and basements and, most importantly, the great platform that is popularly called the 'Mahanavami Platform' [Fig. XII; Ph. 15]. It is a unique monument of ascending levels, built in four stages from the fourteenth to the sixteenth centuries. The sides of the platform are adorned with sculpted slabs depicting a

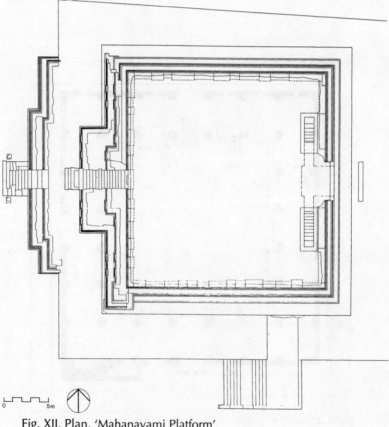

0   5m

Fig. XII. Plan, 'Mahanavami Platform'

Photo 14. Stepped tank (the 'Mahanavami Platform' is in the background)

Photo 15. 'Mahanavami Platform'

variety of courtly scenes: hunting, performances of music and dance, wrestling matches, processions of soldiers, horses, elephants, and even camels. The schist slabs of the fourth phase, on the western side, are the most intricately carved. Steps on the west and east sides lead to the top of the structure. It is not definitively known for which courtly rituals this monument was once used. It is generally presumed that it was from here that the king and his entourage watched the Mahanavami festivities. Another opinion is that this structure was used for coronation ceremonies. Initially, it may even have served as an audience hall.

Ramachandra temple [see **Ph. C**]

The Ramachandra temple [**Fig. XIII**], locally mentioned as the Hazara Rama temple, was the private place of worship for the Vijayanagara kings. It was built in the early fifteenth century, probably by Devaraya I. The temple faces an open space where many of the principal roads of the city converged. To the east of the temple is a lamp column and a small shrine that once probably housed the image of Hanuman.

The temple stands within a walled enclosure. The exterior wall is unique at the site as it is decorated with bands of sculpture. The external face of the enclosure wall contains five friezes of courtly scenes: processions of elephants, horses, soldiers, dancers and musicians, with royal figures within pavilions depicted as watching these parades. Entry into the temple is through doorways on the east and north sides and a smaller door on the south side. On the inner face of the wall, between the north and east gateways, are panels of relief carvings of the entire story of the *Ramayana*. The whole epic is carved once again in three tiers on the outer walls of the mandapa of the principal shrine; the first important panel being that of the fire sacrifice of king Dasharatha (north-end of the west wall). The series ends with the enthronement of Rama (south-end of the west wall).

The main shrine consists of an eight-pillar porch, a rangamandapa, with porches to the east, north and south, two antechambers and a sanctuary. The interior is fairly plain, except for the four black stone pillars of the mandapa which are brilliantly polished and

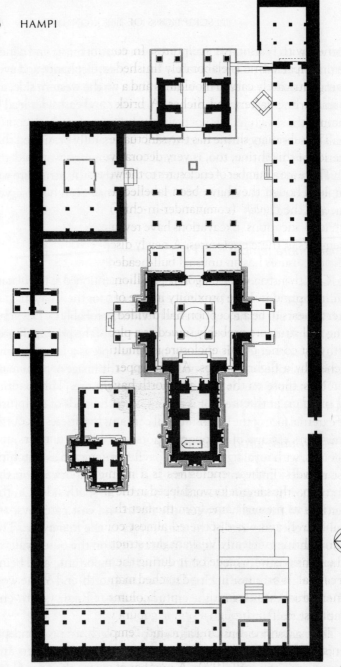

Fig. XIII. Plan, Ramachandra Temple

adorned with Vaishnava sculptures. In contrast, the exterior of the principal shrine is elaborately finished with a high basement having intricately carved mouldings and a wall surface with reliefs separated by pilasters and niches. A brick tower rises above the sanctuary.

The subsidiary shrine has two sanctuaries and a mandapa. The exterior of this shrine, too, is very decorative.

There are a number of enclosures to the west of the Ramachandra temple. Though they have been labelled as the 'mint' and 'residence of the *danaik*' (commander-in-chief) there is no basis for such identifications. Excavations have revealed a number of palace basements in these enclosures. A newly discovered tank in one of these enclosures has an unusual bull-headed water spout.

The two-storeyed octagonal pavillion and the nine-domed pavillion stand in close proximity in one of these enclosures. The latter appears to be a reception hall divided into vaulted bays. The octagonal structure probably served as a pleasure pavillion. In the northwest corner of this enclosure is a multi-domed watch tower, reached by a flight of steps. At the upper level are four domed chambers; those on the west and north have projecting balconies supported on brackets.

'Underground' Virupaksha temple

To the west of these enclosures is a monument dedicated to Virupaksha, the same deity worshipped in the great temple at Hampi. It derives its present name from the fact that it is now below the ground level and was discovered almost completely buried. The original shrine is an early Vijayanagara structure. Various additions and extensions were made on it during the period the site served as a capital. Worth visiting is a detached mandapa in the southwest corner, which has elegantly sculpted columns. The Underground Temple is entered through a simple gopura without a brick tower.

To the north of the Underground Temple is the area that has been termed the Noblemen's Quarters, where excavations are in progress since the early 1980s. A number of palace basements and the remains of three shrines are visible in this area.

Photo 16. Palace basement, in the 'Zenana Enclosure'

Returning to the Ramachandra temple, the path continues some 150 metres north until it arrives at the so-called 'Zenana Enclosure' [**Ph. 16**]. This name is derived from the fact that it is surrounded by high walls, supposedly to protect the privacy of the royal women. Despite its present nomenclature, it is more likely that the structures here were connected with the public, courtly activities of the king than with his private, domestic life. Within the enclosure are the remains of two palace basements, one of which is in the centre of a now empty tank, three watch towers (one square, the second octagonal and the third ruined), a vaulted rectangular structure, and the two-storeyed pavilion. [see **Ph. D**]

The vaulted structure in the northwest corner of the enclosure is sometimes referred to as the guards' quarters. The lack of adequate openings, however, indicates that it is more likely that this was a treasury or storehouse, or it may even have served as a gymnasium.

The two-storeyed pavillion, commonly termed as the 'Lotus Mahal' [**Ph. 17**], is one of the best preserved of all the courtly structures at Vijayanagara. Standing on a basement with fine mouldings, it is laid out symmetrically, with projections in the middle of each side. The building has openings framed by cusped arches, overhung by

Photo 17. 'Lotus Mahal'

curved eaves. A staircase provides access to the upper level. The pavillion is roofed by nine pyramidal towers. Traces of the original stucco decorations that once adorned this building can still be seen.

A doorway in the east wall of the 'Zenana Enclosure' leads to the Elephant Stables [Ph. 18], the most impressive courtly structure at the site. The stables consist of eleven chambers, roofed with alternating domes and twelve-sided vaults, arranged symmetrically on either side of a raised upper chamber for drummers and musicians. The exterior of the stables is dominated by arched openings and wall recesses. The stables probably housed elephants used on state occasions.

The stables face west on to an open space that may have served as a parade ground. The rectangular structure on the north side has a raised arcaded verandah that may have been used for viewing the activities in the open space. The internal court would have been suitable for martial exercises. This structure is sometimes referred to as the 'Guards' Barracks'. The remains of a great gateway define the west side of the open space.

To the south of the 'Zenana Enclosure' are two temples. One of these is the Ellamma temple, which is now below the ground level. Dedicated to a local goddess, this is the only shrine in the 'royal centre' where worship is still conducted. The second is the so-called Ranga temple, which according to an inscription within is dedicated to Madhava, a form of Vishnu. The Madhava temple comprises two shrines and associated columned halls. One of these is plain, the other more elaborately executed.

Temples to the east of the Elephant stables

Here is found a group of Hindu and Jaina shrines that once lined one of the principal roads of the city. There is one medium-sized Vishnu temple, a Shiva shrine, and two Jaina temples. One of the latter has a long and interesting inscription in it, stating that it was built by Devaraya II in 1426 and was dedicated to the Jaina tirthankara Parshvanatha.

Photo 18. Elephant stables

Suburban Centres

Anegondi

Situated on the opposite bank of the Tungabhadra, Anegondi was an important settlement prior to the foundation of Vijayanagara. It continued to be the seat of the royal family after the destruction of Vijayanagara.

Crossing the river at Talarighat, the way to Anegondi starts at the monumental gate near the river, from where a path leads towards the town, a kilometre to the north. The path passes by a dilapidated *matha*, with re-used schist columns and traces of paintings on the ceiling. A little further on are the stone walls with post-Vijayanagara circular bastions that encircle the town.

The dilapidated palace in the heart of Anegondi was built not earlier than the seventeenth or eighteenth century. The main square of the town is dominated by the Gagan Mahal, which resembles the 'Lotus Mahal' to a certain extent. It is now the seat of the town council. Facing the Gagan Mahal is the Ranganatha temple, the principal shrine of Anegondi. The earliest dated temple in the town is the Jaina shrine, built in 1402, by the same patron who constructed the Ganagitti temple. Immediately in front of the Jaina temple are the remains of a later Chalukyan temple, of which the elaborately executed schist doorway is all that survives.

Anegondi's citadel is located one kilometre to the west of the town. The rocky hill is ringed by massive walls. Fortified gates protected by round bastions give access to enclosures with wells, barracks, and other military structures. Further northwest of Anegondi is Pampa Sarovar and Anjenadri Hill.

Kamalapuram

This village is situated immediately to the south of the 'urban core'. A fort, only part of which dates from the Vijayanagara times, once stood in the middle of the village; but it is now mostly demolished. The site Archaeological Museum (open on all days, except Friday, from 10.00 am to 5.00 pm) is well worth a visit. It houses an open-air model of Vijayanagara that gives an excellent idea of the layout of the site. There are galleries in the museum with Shaiva, Vaishnava and other miscellaneous sculptures and also coins and inscriptions. Numerous *sati* [Ph. 19] and hero stones (stone slabs commemorating women who immolated themselves on the death of their husbands and men who died in action) and other sculptures are placed in the gardens of the museum.

The Pattabhirama temple complex is situated to the northeast of Kamalapuram, a short distance from the domed gate, which is

Photo 19.
Sati-stone,
Archaeologi-
cal Museum

in the southeast part of the fortifications around the 'urban core'. [Ph. 20] The Pattabhirama temple has inscriptions dating from the period of Achyutaraya. It used to enshrine the deity Raghunatha. The temple consists of a principal shrine, a subsidiary shrine and a hundred-pillared hall, all standing within a vast rectangular courtyard with a gopura on the east and smaller entrances on the south and north sides.

Kadirampuram

This village is located to the west of the 'urban core'. A Muslim community once lived here, as is indicated by two tombs that can be assigned to the early fifteenth century, and by clusters of gravestones.

Malpannagudi

This village is situated on the road linking Hampi and Kamalapuram with Hospet. Evidently Malpannagudi was a settlement of some importance during the Vijayanagara times as two gateways still stand at either end of the village, one of these now serving as a garage for the temple chariot. The only Vijayanagara period monument in this village is the Mallikarjuna temple, which stands within a square compound, entered on the west through a gopura facing the main road.

An inscription on a slab placed in front of the temple, dated 1412, mentions the construction of a well. Probably the reference is to the stepped well located about 500 metres southwest of the village, beside the road to Hospet.

Anantashayanagudi

This village, 1.5 kilometres, to the northwest of Hospet on the Hampi-Kamalapuram-Hospet road, was once a suburb built by Krishnadevaraya. The modern village got its name from the Vishnu temple, erected by the king in 1524. The monument stands in a walled compound, entered from the west through a large gopura, of

Photo 20. Domed gate

which only the lower granite portion is extant. The Anantashayana temple consists of a large mandapa, open only in the front, a narrow rectangular antechamber and a rectangular sanctum. The long pedestal within the sanctum was intended for a very large image of reclining Vishnu. The tower over the sanctuary, more than twenty-four metres in height, is roofed with an unusual vaulted, double-apsidal-ended roof.

Nagenahali

This modern village was also a part of the suburb built by Krishnadevaraya. It is off the main road. There are two temples here from the Vijayanagara period, one dedicated to Vishnu and the other to Shiva.

Hospet

This town is the largest in the vicinity. In the early sixteenth century, Krishnadevaraya laid out a settlement in the proximity of modern Hospet. Today nothing survives of this suburb. Two tombs in the southern part of Hospet, however, suggests the presence of a Muslim community dating back to the Vijayanagara period.

FIVE

Hampi as an Archaeological Site

Scholarly investigations at Hampi only began after the area came under the British control. The first modern account of the site is provided by the antiquarian Colonel Colin Mackenzie, who later became the Surveyor-General of India, and visited the site in 1799–1800. He described the overall layout and attempted to identify various structures, irrigation works, and fortifications. Sketches and water colours were made of certain monuments, and a survey map of the site was also prepared. The earliest known photographs of the Hampi monuments were of those taken by Colonel Alexander Greenlaw in 1856. These photographs were virtually unknown till 1980 when about sixty waxed-paper negatives came to the notice of scholars. Greenlaw's photographs reveal architectural features that have since disappeared from certain monuments.

The earliest conservation work at the site was undertaken by Major Cole, who was appointed for three years (1881–3) as Conservator of Ancient Monuments. Archaeological survey was taken up after 1885, when the British Government amalgamated the work of conservation along with those of survey and set up five survey areas. Alexander Rea, surveyor of the Madras Survey, stayed for some months at Hampi. He made an attempt to identify buildings and enclosures. The terms used to designate the monuments today, such as 'the mint', 'palace of the danaik' and others were assigned by him; based on his conclusions on the description of the city given by Abdur Razzak.

Sustained epigraphical work at the site commenced with the setting up of the Madras Epigraphical Department in 1887. The summaries of the inscriptions from the principal temples of Hampi began to appear in the *Annual Reports on South Indian Epigraphy*, published from 1887 onwards. The full texts of these records were provided in the volumes of *South Indian Inscriptions*. The series known as *Epigraphia Indica* also carried some of the Hampi epigraphs.

In 1900 Robert Sewell published his seminal work, *A Forgotten Empire*. This was the earliest attempt at a comprehensive picture of the kingdom and its capital. Most valuable in it are Sewell's translations of the accounts of Domingo Paes and Fernao Nuniz.

There was, at the same time, a renewed enthusiasm for archaeological work at the site, facilitated by the reconstitution of the Archaeological Survey and the appointment of John Marshall as its Director-General early in 1902. At this time it was decided that a princely sum of not less than one hundred thousand rupees would be spent per annum for a period of years for archaeological sites of special importance and magnitude. In the Southern Circle, the maximum work done under this scheme was at Vijayanagara. The aim of A.Rea and his successor, A.H.Longhurst, was that of opening up 'the whole site by clearing away the jungle and constructing roads to various buildings, and, further to carry out systematic structural repairs to the buildings'. It was during this time that names such as 'Lotus Mahal', 'Queen's Bath', 'Guards' Quarters', and 'Zenana Enclosure' came to be assigned to the buildings and enclosures that had been referred to by different terms previously. In 1917, the first official guide-book on the site, Longhurst's *Hampi Ruins: Described and Illustrated*, was published. By the end of the 1920s, Hampi could no longer be deemed either as forgotten or ignored. With the construction of roads at the site and the commencement of a bus service between the Hospet station and Hampi, it was no longer inaccessible.

The period between the late 1920s and the early 1970s was a lean one for Vijayanagara scholarship, with conservation and restoration work being reduced to a minimum. The most important task carried out by the Archaeological Survey during this period was the collecting of the sculptures lying in the ruins. This work gathered momentum in the early 1950s with the construction of the Tungabhadra Dam for it was because of this dam and the artificial lakes, canals, and hydro-electric projects connected with it that some areas of the site and its environs were in danger of inundation. The hundreds of sculptures thus collected were eventually housed in the site museum constructed in the early 1970s. Tungabhadra Dam has, unquestionably, brought greater prosperity to this area, but it has also caused irreparable damage to its already fragile heritage. Not only has a part of the site been permanently lost, but many Vijayanagara- period archaeological and architectural features have been obliterated, owing to the tremendous increase in agriculture made possible by the irrigational facilities provided by the dam.

The 1970s witnessed a resurgence of interest in Vijayanagara. *Hampi*, an excellent and up-to-date guide-book by D.Devakunjari of the Archaeological Survey of India, was published. The renewed scholarly research at the site was pioneered by Vasundhara and Pierre-Sylvain Filliozat of the French Institute of Indian Studies, Pondicherry. Through the 1970s, they devoted themselves to examining Vijayanagara architecture, sculpture, iconography, and epigraphs.

The year 1975 marks a watershed in Vijayanagara studies, for it was in that year that the then Union Minister for Education, Professor Nurul Hasan, a noted historian and archaeologist, initi-ated a programme of national projects at three medieval sites—Hampi, Fatehpur-Sikri, and Champaner—in order to expose their city remains and patterns. The work undertaken since 1975 has been multi-faceted in nature: a continuation of the type of activity begun since the end of the last century, such as the clearance and conservation, together with epigraphical studies, and an added di-mension of excavation, surface archaeology, and publication on a scale never embarked upon before. This work at Hampi has been carried out by the Archaeological Survey of India, the Karnataka

State Directorate of Archaeology and Museums as well as the scholars of the Vijayanagara Research Project under the direction of John Fritz and George Michell.

Excavations have been carried out by the Archaeological Survey in the 'Royal Enclosure', the area to the east of the Ramachandra temple, the 'Mint Enclosure,' and other places. The most important area that the State Directorate had taken up for excavation is the large zone to the north of the 'Underground Temple', which has been termed, for the sake of convenience, as the 'Noblemen's Quarters'. Both the archaeological departments have engaged on an ambitious scheme of clearance and conservation, both of standing and exposed structures. The most controversial conservation project was the one involving the magnificent Narasimha monolith, which was begun in the 1980s, when the Archaeological Survey decided to restore it to its original form. Fierce criticism that the work being undertaken was going beyond the limits of conservation to that of a total reconstruction of the sculpture led to the work being suspended mid-way, leaving this famous image in a rather sorry state.

An important contribution made by the staff of the State Directorate of Archaeology has been their widespread exploration of the site, not only to identify hitherto unnoticed structures and sculptures, but also to locate unpublished inscriptions, resulting in the publication of over 260 epigraphs. The Directorate has undertaken the *Vijayanagara: Progress of Research* series, publication of which is going on.

The Vijayanagara Research Project has brought to Hampi since 1980 the participation of a team of international and Indian scholars. The general aim of the Vijayanagara Research Project has been to document the physical remains of this settlement as they are visible on the surface, using the techniques of surface archaeology, so as to understand the life of this city as the capital of the most powerful Hindu state in the pre-modern south India. Mapping of the entire site, architectural drawings of all standing structures and extensive publications, especially under the *Vijayanagara Research Monograph Series*, has been a major contribution of this team.

An extension of the programme of surface archaeology undertaken in the core area of the city by the Vijayanagara Research Project was the Vijayanagara Metropolitan Survey, carried on for a decade since 1987 under the direction of Carla Sinopoli and Kathleen Morrison. This survey was aimed at an understanding of the city of Vijayanagara within its regional context of the metropolitan area that supplied it with food, raw materials, labour, and craft products. A systematic survey was made of the 'greater metropolitan area', a zone of some 650 square kilometres from the capital to its outer-most fortifications.

By the end of the twentieth century, Vijayanagara had definitely been resurrected, both for scholars and for the general public. Hampi was placed by the UNESCO on its list of 'World Heritage Monuments' in recognition of the global importance of the site.

If the first phase of the opening up of the site in the first quarter of the twentieth century made it known in the scholarly circles in India, the second phase in the last quarter of the century has made Hampi-Vijayanagara better known and popular with both Indian as well as foreign visitors and tourists. This was possible because of a growth in accommodation facilities. If prior to 1975, except for the Inspection Bungalow at Kamalapuram, no accommodation was available at the site itself, now the Karnataka State Tourism Corporation's three-star hotel at Kamalapuram and a number of lodges at Hampi have sprung up. In recent years, autorickshaws have begun to ply at the site and telephone and even fax and internet facilities are easily available. The construction of a broad-gauge railway line to Hospet in the 1980s has resulted in a direct train service from Bangalore to Hospet; and very recently, luxury bus services have begun to connect Hampi directly to Goa. In 1997, the construction of a concrete bridge across the Tungabhadra at Talarighat was started. If completed, this would open up the site to more vehicular traffic and further endanger the already fragile heritage of the site. However, the work on the bridge has been suspended due to strong protests from the archaeologists and environmentalists. Again, prior to 1970, the main books on Hampi were those by R. Sewell and A.H. Longhurst, both of which, though valuable pioneering works, have become outdated. At present, a wealth of written material and good tourist maps are readily available.

Thus, by the end of the twentieth century, Hampi-Vijayanagara had become a well-known archaeological site, both in scholarly circles as well as on the tourist beat. This opening up of Hampi has been a mixed blessing: On the one hand, it has become well-known and accessible, on the other hand the increase in development and tourism has brought in its wake new and serious hazards to the site and its monuments.

Appendix
List of Kings Who Ruled from Vijayanagara

Sangama Dynasty (1336–1485)

1. Harihara I (1336–56)
2. Bukka I (1356–77)
3. Harihara II (1377–1404)
4. Virupaksha I
5. Bukka II
6. Devaraya I (1406–22)
7. Ramachandra
8. Vira Vijaya
9. Devaraya II (1424–46)
10. Mallikarjuna (1446–65)
11. Virupaksha II (1465–85)

Saluva Dynasty (1485–1505)

1. Saluva Narasimha (1485–91)
2. Timma
3. Immadi Narasimha (1491–1505) ⎤ Regency of Narasa Nayaka
⎦ and Vira Narasimha

Tuluva Dynasty (1505–70)

1. Vira Narasimha (1505–9)
2. Krishnadevaraya (1509–29)
3. Achyutaraya (1529–42)
4. Sadashiva (1542–65)
   (Regency of Ramaraya)

Practical Tips and Information

The best time to visit Hampi is between early November and the end of February. During this season, it is fairly cold at night, though the days can be warm. Every year, a cultural festival is held at Hampi between 3 and 5 November. For those who wish to witness a religious festival and chariot ceremonies, the rituals that draw vast local crowds are the Phalapuja and the Kalyanotsava celebrations of the Virupaksha temple, that fall during the months of December and March-April respectively.

The site is very extensive and it would be advisable to spend at least two days at Hampi. For those who are energetic, the monuments can be visited on foot. However, if one does not have one's own conveyance, it would be more advisable to rent a bicycle, an autorickshaw, or a tourist taxi. The Karnataka State Tourist Development Corporation conducts a one-day bus tour of the Hampi monuments and T.B. Dam, starting from the Tourist office at Hospet (Regional Tourist office, Rotary Circle, Hospet; Telephone: 28537). Tourist guides are also available. They can be contacted through the Tourist office at Hospet or at Hampi (in the Hampi bazaar).

There are direct luxury bus services between Hampi and Goa. Via Goa, there are also bus links between Hampi and Mumbai, Pune, and other cities. Bus tickets and even train and air tickets can be arranged through travel agents at Hampi or Hospet. The nearest airports are at Belgaum, 259 kilometres away, or Bangalore, at a distance of 325 kilometres. The nearest railway station is Hospet Junction, thirteen kilometres from Hampi. There are direct train services connecting Hospet with Bangalore, Hubli, Miraj, and Guntakal. Passengers travelling by train from Delhi, Mumbai, Chennai etc. are advised to alight at Guntakal to catch a train to Hospet.

Trains from Guntakal to Hospet and then on to Hubli:

No.303: departure from Guntakal at 21.30; arrival at Hospet at 1.30

No.7225 Amaravati Express: departure from Guntakal at 8.00; arrival at Hospet 10.45

Trains (starting from Hubli) connecting Hospet to Guntakal:

No.304: arrival at Hospet at 2.45, departure at 2.55; arrival at Guntakal at 6.15

No.7226 Amaravati Express: arrival at Hospet at 16.00, departure at 16.10; arrival at Guntakal at 18.20

Other trains:

No.6592 Hampi Express connects Bangalore with Hubli, via Guntakal and Hospet: departure from Bangalore at 22.00; reaches Guntakal at 5.00; reaches Hospet at 7.50; arrival at Hubli at 11.00

No.6591 Hampi Express connects Hubli with Bangalore, via Hospet and Guntakal: departure from Hubli at 17.00; reaches Hospet at 20.00; reaches Guntakal at 22.20; arrival at Bangalore at 6.25

No.312 from Miraj to Hospet: arrival at Hospet at 12.15

No.311 from Hospet to Miraj: departure from Hospet at 15.55

Hospet is connected by road with all the major cities of India as National Highway 13 passes through it. Two state highways (Hubli-Raichur and Raichur-Harihara) also pass through Hospet.

There are no major tourist sites very close to Hampi. The nearest are the Chalukyan sites of Aihole (146 kilometres), Badami (180 kilometres), and Pattadakal. The later-Chalukyan temples in and around Gadag (98 kilometres) are not too far from the site.

Accommodation/restaurants/shops at Hampi:

There are no sizable hotels in Hampi village itself. There are, however, a number of lodges and guest-houses. Of these, Shanti, Rahul, and Shambhu guest-houses are the most suitable. Rates for a room range from Rs 100 to Rs 450 per day. Considering that the first toilet was constructed at Hampi only in 1989 and that till the early 1990s there was no accommodation suitable for visitors in the village, it is indeed a great development that there are now over 300 rooms available at Hampi, though the facilities are rather basic in all these local lodges. During the 'season' advance booking is recommended.

During the last few years a number of restaurants have sprung up in Hampi village serving both south Indian as well as north Indian and even continental food!

There are also a number of shops, mainly catering to tourists. 'Aspiration Stores' stocks a wide variety of books, postcards, and stationery. For brass knick-knacks and old coins one could visit the stall run by V.S.Kotreshi.

Addresses:

Shanthi Guest House
River Road, Hampi 583 211
Phone: (08394) 41568

Rahul Guest House
Hampi 583 229
Phone: (08394) 41648

Shambhu Guest House
Hampi 583 211
Phone: (08394) 41610

Aspiration Stores
Hampi 583 239
Phone: (08394) 41254

V.S.Kotreshi
Numismatist
Hampi 583 239
Phone: (08394) 41559

Vijay Travels
Tourist Information Centre
Hampi;
Phone (08394) 41304

Accommodation in Government guest-houses and hotels:

The visitor to Hampi could seek accommodation in the Inspection Bungalow at Kamalapuram, an old temple that has been converted into a two-bedroom guest-house. For this accommodation one would need to contact the Assistant Engineer, PWD, No.2 Sub-division, Hospet, Phone (08394) 28754. The Tungabhadra Dam (seventeen kilometres from Hampi) and the Hampi Power House Camp (H.P.C., three kilometres from Kamalapuram) also have guest-houses. The arrangements for stay in these have to be made with the engineer of the Irrigation Department (Superintending Engineer, H.E.S., T.B. Board, T.B. Dam). The one disadvantage of these guest-houses is that they cater primarily to government officials. A private person is liable to be asked to vacate the room, without notice, if a government guest arrives!

As far as the hotels are concerned, the three-star Hotel Mayura Bhuvaneshwari at Kamalpuram, run by K.S.T.D.C. (Karnataka State Tourist Development Corporation), is recommended since it is within easy reach of the monuments. It has thirty-two rooms; and a new Yatri-Nivas, providing cheaper accommodation, is under construction. Bookings have to be done in advance at the headquarters of the K.S.T.D.C. in Bangalore.

In Hospet there are a number of hotels and lodges; the Kartik, Malligi, Priyadarshini, Shanbag, and Nagarjuna are recommended.

Addresses:

Hotel Mayura Bhuvaneshwari
Kamalapura 583 221
Phone (08394) 41574

Head Office
K.S.T.D.C.
10/4 Kasturba Road
Queen's Circle
Bangalore 560 001
Phone (080) 2212901
Fax (080) 2272580/2238016

Hotel Karthik
S.P. Road, Patel Nagar
Hospet 583 201
Phones (08394) 24938/
25639; Fax (08394) 20028

Hotel Malligi
6/143, J.N. Road,
Off Hampi Road
Hospet 538 201
Phone (08394) 28101;
Fax (08394) 27038

Hotel Priyadarshini
Station Road
Hospet 583 201
Phones (08394) 28838/
28096/28139/27017/27313;
Fax (08394) 24709

Shanbag Towers International
College Road
Hospet 538 201
Phones (08394) 25910 to
25918; Fax (08394) 25919

Hotel Nagarjuna Residency
Patel Nagar
Hospet 583 201
Phones (08394) 29009

Glossary

Acharya	:	teacher, preceptor. Shri-Vaishnavas acknowledge a line of such preceptors
Alvar	:	Shri-Vaishnava saint. There are twelve *alvars* who are venerated by the Shri-Vaishnavas
Anjaneya	:	another name of Hanuman
antarala	:	antechamber
Anantashayana	:	one of the reclining forms of Vishnu
Bhairava	:	'Terrible'. Name of one of the fierce aspects of Shiva
chakra	:	'Discus, wheel'. A weapon; one of the attributes of Vishnu
Chandrashekhara	:	an aspect of Shiva having the crescent moon as a head ornament
Daksha	:	father of Sati (Shiva's consort). His head was cut off by Virabhadra; later he was brought back to life with a ram's head
Dakshinamurti	:	'The southern image'. A peaceful form of Shiva as the supreme teacher
Dasharatha	:	king of Ayodhya, father of Rama
Devi	:	goddess
Dharma	:	Moral or religious duty; law; custom

Durga	:	a militant goddess, who combats demons who threaten the stability of the universe. Later Durga became linked with Shiva
Ganesha	:	the elephant-headed son of Shiva and Parvati. He is regarded as the remover of obstacles and as the god of wisdom
garbhagriha	:	'Womb-house', the sanctuary in a temple
Garuda	:	the mythical eagle, the vehicle of Vishnu
gopura	:	ornamented, pyramidal entrance gateway to a south Indian temple
Hanuman	:	the monkey-chief, who helped Rama rescue Sita
Kalyana-mandapa	:	'Wedding-hall'. A special pavilion in a temple in which the ceremonial wedding of the god and goddess is celebrated annually
Kalyanotsava	:	annual marriage-festival of the god and goddess
Kama/Kama-deva	:	presiding deity of love, especially sexual love
Kishkindha	:	a legendary monkey kingdom in south India
Krishna	:	the eighth and the most popular incarnation of Vishnu
Lakshmana	:	a younger brother of Rama
Lakshmi	:	consort of Vishnu, goddess of fortune and prosperity
Lakshmi-Narasimha	:	representation of Vishnu as Narasimha together with Lakshmi who is seated on his left thigh
linga	:	phallus, a symbol of the male principle. The *linga* is worshipped as a symbol of Shiva
Mahamandapa/Maharangamandapa	:	'Great hall'. Frontal pillared-hall of a temple
Mahanavami	:	Nine-day festival, also known as *Navaratri*
Maharajadhiraja	:	'King of kings'
Mahishasura	:	buffalo-demon who is ultimately killed by Durga
Mallikarjuna	:	a form of Shiva, especially worshipped at Srisailam in Andhra Pradesh
mandapa	:	open or closed pillared hall
matha	:	monastery, cloister, college
Meru	:	a mythical mountain reputed to be at the centre of the universe
Naga	:	snake
Nandi	:	name of the white bull of Shiva
Narasimha	:	man-lion; the fourth incarnation of Vishnu

Parvati	:	daughter of the mountain (Himalaya). She is the gracious, friendly aspect of Shiva's consort
Phalapuja	:	festival of the betrothal of Virupaksha and Pampa
prakara	:	courtyard
Rama/Ramachandra/ Raghunatha	:	the hero of the *Ramayana*. The seventh incarnation of Vishnu
Ramanuja	:	a devotee of Vishnu, founder of the Vishishtad-vaita philosophical system and of Shri-Vaishnavism
Ramayana	:	'Rama's career'. A famous epic in seven books dealing with the adventures of Rama
rangamandapa	:	enclosed pillared-hall with four openings
Ranganatha	:	one of the reclining forms of Vishnu
Ravana	:	the ten-headed chief of the demons who ruled over Lanka
Raya	:	king
ratha-vidhi	:	chariot-street
Sarasvati	:	goddess of knowledge, learning and speech
Sati	:	'Good, faithful wife'. The wife who immolates herself following the death of her husband. Sati is also one of the names of Shiva's consort
Sita	:	wife of Rama. She was abducted by Ravana and held captive in Lanka
Shiva	:	auspicious. Shiva is usually included in the Hindu triad as the 'destroyer' along with Brahma, the creator and Vishnu, the preserver
Shri-Vaishnavas	:	Vaishnava brahmins of southern India, followers of Ramanuja's philosophy
shukanasi	:	inner antechamber
sthalapurana	:	text that recounts the mythic origin and traditions of a sacred spot or temple
Subrahmanya	:	the second son of Shiva. He is the commander-in-chief of the divine armies
Sugriva	:	king of the monkeys; brother of Vali
Surya	:	Sun-god
Surya-Narayana	:	composite image, half Surya and half Narayana (a form of Vishnu)
Tirtha	:	'Bathing place, passage'. A shrine or sacred bathing place; a place of pilgrimage

Tirthankara(s)	:	'Ford-finder' , Saviour. Term associated with the twenty-four Jaina teachers
Tirumangai	:	one of the *alvars*
Tiruvengalanatha	:	a form of Vishnu, worshipped at the famous temple at Tirumalai-Tirupati
vahana	:	vehicle, mount of a deity. The animal on which the deity rides
Vali	:	monkey-king, brother of Sugriva
Varaha	:	'Boar'. The third incarnation of Vishnu
Venkateshavara	:	same as Tiruvengalanatha
Virabhadra	:	an emanation of Shiva, who was created in order to destroy Daksha's sacrifice
Virashaiva/Lingayat	:	a Shaiva sect founded by Basava
Vishnu	:	all-prevading. The preserver of the universe, a member of the Hindu triad consisting of Brahma, Vishnu, and Shiva
Vitthala	:	a form of Vishnu especially worshipped at Pandharpur (Maharashtra)
yali	:	mythical composite beast
yantra	:	mystic diagram

Bibliographic Guide

This book provides merely an introduction to Hampi. Further reading would give the interested visitor information on the varied aspects of this fascinating site.

The volume by Robert Sewell, *A Forgotten Empire*, Reprint (New Delhi: Asian Educational Services, 1984) is still of great value, although it was first published in 1900. Of special interest are the travel accounts of Paes and Nuniz that are included in it. A.H. Longhurst's *Hampi Ruins: Described and Illustrated*, Reprint (New Delhi: Asian Education Services, 1982) is of significance since it is the first guide-book on the site. A more up to date and informative guide-book is D. Devakunjari's *Hampi*, Third Edition (New Delhi: Archaeological Survey of India, 1992). This book can be purchased at the site Archaeological Museum, Kamalapuram. If the reader is able to lay hands on it, the *Marg* volume on Hampi makes for interesting reading: G. Michell and V. Filliozat (eds), *Splendours of the Vijayanagara Empire: Hampi* (Bombay: Marg Publications, 1981). Those who like visuals would be fascinated by the pictorial book *Vijayanagara: Through the Eyes of Alexander J.Greenlaw 1856 and John Gollings 1983*, edited by M.S. Nagaraja Rao (Mysore: Directorate of Archaeology and Museums, 1988). The most comprehensive volume on the site and the best illustrated one is, undoubtedly, *City of Victory—Vijayanagara*, by J. Gollings, J.M. Fritz and G.Michell (New York: Aperture Foundation, 1991).

There are works of a more specialized nature that deal with one or other facet of the site. All in the list given below, except the first two and the last, are publications of the Vijayanagara Research Project:

Filliozat, P-S. and Filliozat, V., *Hampi-Vijayanagar: The Temple of Vithala* (New Delhi: Sitaram Bhartia Institute of Scientific Research, 1988).

Michell, G., *Architectural Inventory of the Urban Core*, 2 Vols. (Mysore: Directorate of Archaeology and Museums, 1990).

Dallapiccola, A.L., Fritz, J.M., Michell, G., and Rajasekhara, S., *The Ramachandra Temple at Vijayanagara* (New Delhi: Manohar Publications and the American Institute of Indian Studies, 1991).

Michell, G., *The Vijayanagara Courtly Style: Incorporation and Synthesis in the Royal Architecture of Southern India* (New Delhi: Manohar Publications and the American Institute of Indian Studies, 1992).

Verghese, Anila, *Religious Traditions at Vijayanagara: As Revealed Through Its Monuments* (New Delhi: Manohar Publications and the American Institute of Indian Studies, 1995).

Dallapiccola, Anna and Verghese, Anila, *Sculpture at Vijayanagara: Iconography and Style* (New Delhi: Manohar Publications and the American Institute of Indian Studies, 1998).

Verghese, Anila, *Archaeology, Art and Religion: New Perspectives on Vijayanagara* (New Delhi: Oxford University Press, 2000).

For a more general study of the Vijayanagara and the post-Vijayanagara art and architecture in the capital and throughout southern India, one could refer to George Michell's, *Architecture and Art of Southern India— Vijayanagara and the Successor States: The New Cambridge History of India* 1.6 (Cambridge: Cambridge University Press, 1995).

In addition to these, there are some forthcoming publications which would add much to the knowledge of Vijayanagara. Noteworthy among these are George Michell's *Architectural Inventory of the Sacred Centre* (New Delhi: Manohar Publications and the Americal Institute of Indian Studies), and *New Lights on Hampi, Marg* volume edited by G. Michell and John M. Fritz (commemorating twenty years of research [1980–2000] conducted at the site).